WOMEN
AT
THE TOP

WOMEN AT THE TOP

WHAT WOMEN UNIVERSITY AND COLLEGE PRESIDENTS SAY ABOUT EFFECTIVE LEADERSHIP

Mimi Wolverton, Beverly L. Bower,
and Adrienne E. Hyle

Routledge
Taylor & Francis Group

NEW YORK AND LONDON

First published in 2009 by Stylus Publishing, LLC.

Published in 2023 by Routledge
605 Third Avenue, New York, NY 10017
4 Park Square, Milton Park, Abingdon, Oxon OX14 4RN

Routledge is an imprint of the Taylor & Francis Group, an informa business.

© 2009 Taylor & Francis Group

Library of Congress Cataloging-in-Publication-Data
Wolverton, Mimi.
 Women at the top : what women university and
college presidents say about effective leadership /
Mimi Wolverton, Beverly L. Bower, and Adrienne E.
Hyle.—1st ed.
  p. cm. — (Pathways to leadership)
 Includes bibliographical references and index.
 ISBN 978–1-57922–255–0 (cloth : alk. paper)—
 ISBN 978–1-57922–256–7 (pbk. : alk. paper)
  1. Women college presidents—United States—
Biography. 2. Educational leadership—United
States. I. Bower, Beverly L. II. Hyle, Adrienne E.
(Adrienne Evans), 1950– III. Title.
 LA2311.W64 2009
 378.0092—dc22
                              2008025795

ISBN: 9781579222567 (pbk)
ISBN: 9781003448778 (ebk)

DOI: 10.4324/9781003448778

To the wonderful women who took time to share their stories with us and to the future women leaders who choose to follow down the road less traveled

CONTENTS

Contents

ACKNOWLEDGMENTS

A special thanks to John von Knorring, our publisher, for believing in the series and the power of storytelling; to Judy Coughlin, our production manager, and the gang at Stylus, for helping bring this book to fruition; and to Wanda Costen, our colleague, for her special contributions to the original research project.

Photograph of Gretchen M. Bataille on page 6 by Angilee Wilkerson; photograph of Mildred Garcia, page 36, by Dennis Trantham/Westside Studio; photograph of Carol C. Harter, page 54, by Geri Kodey, UNLV.

FOREWORD

Pathways to Leadership is a series about successful women who have reached the pinnacle of their careers. This series features stories about extraordinary women who have found paths to success—whether it's leading a college or university or becoming successful scholars in science and engineering or thriving in some other male-dominated arena. We focus on women because even though women constitute more than half of the populace they remain leadership anomalies in many industries.

Women have made inroads into the top leadership ranks in business, government, and higher education, but progress has been slow. In 2006, only ten of the Fortune 500 businesses and twenty of the Fortune 1000 firms had women CEOs. Similar patterns persist for elected government positions. In the 107th (2007) U.S. Congress, thirteen women served in the Senate and sixty-one in the House. In the history of this country, only twenty-nine women have been state governors; in 2007, eight held that title.

In male-dominated academic fields, including all major hard sciences, math, and engineering, a comparable situation exists. Even though the number of women completing Ph.D.s in these fields is up, women fill few tenured or tenure-track positions. In 2006, just over 15% of social and behavioral sciences and less than 15% of life sciences full professors were women, despite the fact that 30% and 20%, respectively, of the earned doctorates in these fields in the last thirty years were awarded to women. As recently as 2007, reports cited engineering as the most male-dominated field of study, with men filling more than 90% of the full-time faculty positions. Sixty percent of the women with doctoral degrees in engineering said they planned to pursue postgraduate academic positions; yet, just over 17% of all junior faculty were women.

The college and university presidency is little better. In "Same Look, Different Decade," a 2007 article in the *Chronicle of Higher Education*, the author states, "The remarkable thing about the profile of the typical college president—a married, graying White man with a doctoral degree—is how little it has changed over the last 20 years." Eighty-six percent of presidents in 2006 were White and 77% of them were male, with the majority of women presidents heading small, private, four-year universities or community colleges.

Women at the Top is the inaugural offering in the **Pathways to Leadership** series. In it, the authors bring to life the stories of nine college and university presidents. All but one woman featured in this book is the first woman to serve as president of her institution. Most of them have careers that encompass a series of firsts. All can be considered early explorers who entered into relatively uncharted territory. One of them, Betty Siegel, the first woman to head a public institution in Georgia—who did so for twenty-five years—might even be considered a true pioneer, having been one of the longest-serving college presidents in the country.

We invite you to join us in celebrating these exceptional women, their lives, and their careers. We hope their stories will inspire others to follow in their footsteps. We assure you they will raise questions about the disparity between men and women that continues to exist in the American college presidency.

Mimi Wolverton, Series Editor
Pathways to Leadership

ONE

WHAT'S IN A STORY?

I SAK DINESEN ONCE SAID, "To be a person is to have a story to tell." Stories explain life. They raise questions, they get us thinking, and they help us see people. Well-told stories render lives memorable.

Storytelling captures our attention and illuminates images we carry within us. Unlike a film, which passively entertains its audience, a story engages us in filling in the gaps. For this reason, stories have the potential for greater influence. They tell us who a person is, why she is where she is, what she wants, what she believes, and how she enlists others in her dreams, desires, and needs.

Women at the Top is a collection of exceptional stories about nine exceptional women—Gretchen M. Bataille, Barbara Douglass, Mildred García, Carol C. Harter, Mamie Howard-Golladay, Martha T. Nesbitt, Pamela Sue Shockley-Zalabak, Betty L. Siegel, and Karen Gayton Swisher. Each confronts her world with grace, her work with passion, and her life with enthusiasm.

Reciprocal trust is a cornerstone of these women's presidencies. Nesbitt suggests that "no one trusts you just because you are president. You build trust." Shockley-Zalabak closed her campus on the word of her police chief because she instinctively trusted his judgment. The basis for such trust is an intricate intertwining of competence, commitment, integrity, and credibility. As Swisher puts it, "You must be credible to survive." Siegel repeatedly talks about the authenticity of leaders. Howard-Golladay states flatly, "If you can't earn trust and credibility, you might as well just hang it up."

All of these women believe that their word is their bond. They are convinced that if you are not passionate about what you do and committed to the institution that employs you, you simply can't do the all-consuming work required of a CEO. Howard-Golladay is her institution's "strongest advocate," not because it is her job, but because she likes advocating for it. Bataille notes, "If you're not passionate about where you are, you shouldn't be there."

Competence goes without question. As Nesbitt succinctly states, "It's not my job to make all the decisions, it's my job to be competent." García contends that "women and people of color have to be 200% better" for others to see them as competent. These women are innovative and entrepreneurial. They take necessary risks. Harter maintains that you must be willing to put yourself out there. For Douglass, risk taking is a safeguard against retrenchment. Shockley-Zalabak believes that you trust "your gut reaction" in balancing the "art and science" of decision making. Time and again, Bataille embraces possibilities only doable through gauging the risks as reasonable and then moving forward.

They favor collaboration. Howard-Golladay observes, "I'm only as good as the team I work with." García declares, "I share power." Siegel contends, "Building the team is probably one of the most important things a president does." They are confident. It's the baseline for García. Although admitting you must have it, Nesbitt refers to confidence as a gray area and cautions that too much keeps you from asking for help when you most need it.

Each woman possesses a healthy dose of ambition, but it is not nearly as strong as her desire to better her organization and make a contribution to others. García and Douglass deliberately set their sights on a presidency but are also passionate about the students they serve. Several of these women didn't aspire to the presidency. "It just happened," confesses Bataille. Swisher is the only one who always took on leadership responsibilities at the request of others but never quite understood why they considered her a leader.

In an old adage, three people are working at a construction site. A passerby asks each one what he is doing. The first man says he is laying bricks; the second man says he is building a wall; but the third man says he is building a cathedral. These women built cathedrals. They breathed life into their visions making them worthy of the struggle it took to achieve them.

Harter went to the University of Nevada, Las Vegas, because she wanted to build a school. Siegel led five different institutions as Kennesaw transitioned from a sleepy little commuter college to Georgia's third-largest university. Swisher was driven by her personal need to give back to the Native American community.

They put their values into action through consistently demonstrating determination, respect for others, and personal honesty and integrity. Along the way, each woman enjoyed the journey in her own way. In fact, Douglass, Siegel, and Nesbitt openly point to fun as a most underrated value. Siegel loves what she does. Douglass lives by the motto, "If it isn't fun, don't do it." Nesbitt advises that a sense of humor goes a long way toward relieving stress. It must, because she thanks God every day that she didn't get a different presidency.

They anticipate. They seem to gauge intuitively what others are thinking. They plan. Harter firmly believes that "you can't stay in the status quo" and "you certainly can't go back to the past." Douglass challenged her people to take their history and work with her toward the future because "what worked in 1982 isn't going to work now." They know the issues. García reads the *New York Times, Harvard Business Review,* and the *Chronicle of Higher Education.* Siegel reads the *Marion Daily Journal* to understand the county, the *Atlantic Journal* to understand the state, and the *New York Times.* Shockley-Zalabak also follows the news and reads broadly; especially in areas, such as globalization, emerging technology, and sustainability.

These women look inward revealing sometimes hard-to-perceive forces that shape their lives; and their story lines tie us to the larger cultural fabric in which they operate. Swisher's Dakota Sioux heritage dominates her approach to life and leadership. Douglass's Peace Corps experiences broadened her definition of and appreciation for the impact of culture on our lives. Howard-Golladay's upbringing in a deeply segregated South made her sensitive to situations in which discrimination puts individuals at a disadvantage. Siegel "owns her roots." Harter's Irish American, New York-bred directness served her well as a leader, but her initial miscalculation of Las Vegas's political culture haunted her presidency.

With one exception, each is the first woman to head her institution. (Douglass followed a woman into the office.) As a consequence, in telling their stories, they help make the invisible visible. They are consummate communicators. Shockley-Zalabak's academic background in organizational communication permeates her approach to leadership. They are storytellers. Siegel proudly claims storytelling as her primary form of communication.

What's in a Story?

Our nine presidents know the power of words, and, in telling their stories, they let us know who they are, what their visions are, and what they value. Their trailblazing courage, and that of other women born to the World War II and Baby Boomer generations, has paved the way for those who choose to follow them into the presidency.

AUTHORS' NOTE

In telling their stories, we combine first- and third-person perspectives. The former lets the reader listen directly to these women. We narrate their stories to move them along, but each woman tells her own story in her own words. Each story's final rendering was created from the individual's personal recollections, speeches, institutional websites, and newspaper and journal articles written about her. We omitted in-text references because we believe they intrude on the story being told. At the end of each chapter we provide a brief bibliographical note highlighting the main resources used in telling that particular story. At the end of the book, we have included a detailed explanation of the research process used to generate these stories.

BIBLIOGRAPHICAL NOTE

Storytelling resources used in this introduction can be found at www.callofstory.org and www.storyteller.net.

TWO

I NEVER MET AN OPPORTUNITY I DIDN'T LIKE

Gretchen M. Bataille
University of North Texas

"A FTER SEVERAL YEARS of lecturing at Iowa State, I knew that I could not continue at a university without a doctorate, so I enrolled in the 'experimental' doctor of arts degree in English at Drake University. I was a single mom. I could not afford to quit my job and go off to graduate school someplace and support my two kids [now both grown and college educated] on an assistantship. My colleagues told me that if I didn't have a Ph.D., I'd never get a job, that a D.A. was a waste of my time. But the opportunity was there and I took advantage of it. It turned out to be a good choice because it included courses that introduced me to higher education while at the same time requiring extensive English courses. I really didn't want to write a dissertation about dead, White men (or White women for that matter), and this program let me explore a new field—Native American literature. The rest is history. I went on to publish fourteen books and numerous book chapters and articles on Native American

literature, diversity, civil rights, and, most recently, on administration. The courses in higher education have served me well as
an administrator. And I've never had any problem getting a job."
Gretchen Bataille was born in Mishawaka, Indiana, in 1944.
Three of her four grandparents were immigrants. Neither her
grandparents nor her parents went to college, but "they knew the
value of hard work. Sitting around was not part of how I grew
up. I had to contribute. As the first born child, in my father's eyes
I was a boy, so I did mostly 'boy' chores, like mowing the grass,
and I worked for him. Dad owned a neighborhood store that had
a soda fountain and sold packaged drugs—aspirin and Alka-Selt-
zer were big sellers.

"He had a soft side, but he was a yeller. 'You didn't do that
right.' Fine, I quit. And I would. Pretty soon, he's, 'Get back here.
You're the best clerk that ever worked for me.' I was very independent, but my parents trusted me, even though at times they
didn't like my independence."

Her experience in the family business taught her to treat people with dignity and respect and to always do her best. These
values still guide her work today.

In high school Gretchen was successful academically—in spite
of working nights and weekends from junior high through high
school. Her friends were primarily students who aspired to attend college. "For me, going to college was doing what my
friends were doing." Her father didn't want her to go to college
and didn't think girls needed to, but she was able to convince her
parents that she should. Her father's requirements were that she
attend a public university in Indiana, study science, and continue
working at the store summers, weekends, and holidays.

She began college at Purdue University with a major in biology, even though her heart wasn't in it. She later switched ma-
jors—first to French and then to English. She left Purdue during

her junior year to get married and moved to California. And, although she didn't plan to go beyond a bachelor's degree, she discovered that in California one more year would give her a master's and a lifetime teaching certificate. In the late 1960s she moved to Iowa State, teaching while her husband completed his Ph.D. Shortly after, she was divorced.

As a consequence, she has been a single mother much of her career. "I worked full time; I did what I needed to do. I had a faculty job for twenty years, and I arranged my schedules around day care, babysitting, school field trips, and going to school. I always did what I felt was best for my children, and for me. Each opportunity I pursued was a 'best decision.' But my going to college made, perhaps, the greatest difference in our lives.

"I didn't follow the model of planning my life that is driven by where you want to be in five or ten years. That can destroy you if you don't make it. The thing about not planning is you're never disappointed. You're always happy about where you are and what you are doing because you're not thinking, oh, my gosh, I'm this old and I haven't become whatever it is I wanted to become. I've never looked for the next job. The next job just sort of found me, and it's been a good fit, and it works.

"I think you always have to do the job you're in, do it well, and not worry about what comes next. That's part of taking advantage of opportunities. I never aspired to be a president. It happened. But it wouldn't have happened if I had not done a good job as a faculty member, as a chair, as a dean, and so on."

Her career reads like a litany of taking advantage of opportunities. She has forty years of teaching experience, from junior high to graduate school, in six different states, and in several academic departments. In each administrative position she continued to teach at least one course a year or serve on graduate student committees, a tradition she continues as president. She has been department chair, dean, provost, and a state system senior vice president. "I have done every administrative job. I know the limitations of being a department chair, but I also know the responsibilities that come with being provost. I can identify with each group.

"I worked under Gary Krahenbuhl at Arizona State University. He's so level-headed, doesn't get dragged down, and gives good advice. He was a great role model for me. He taught me that my personal opinions about an individual are not the basis on which to make a decision about that person's future. I've listened to my colleagues say, 'Oh, I don't like what X says about this' or 'That person really dresses weirdly.' I don't care what people wear. Obviously, I want them to make a good impression if they're in a public environment, but some of the quirkiest people do their jobs and represent the university well. If we were all the same, we wouldn't come up with the creative ideas that can come from people who view the world differently. The questions have to be, can they do the job, have they done the job, do they deserve a salary increase or promotion or whatever? I have to separate any personal feelings about that person. This requirement holds for any administrator—chair, dean, provost, or president."

Gretchen started her administrative career at Iowa State University as the founding chair of the American Indian Studies Program. At Arizona State she served as both department chair and associate dean, followed by provost positions at the University of California, Santa Barbara, and Washington State University. More recently she spent six years as chief academic officer for the sixteen-campus University of North Carolina system with responsibility for close to 200,000 students in a system with two medical schools, a dental school, and schools of veterinary medicine, pharmacy, and public health, among others.

In her years as an administrator, she gained experience in budgeting, personnel management, planning, fund-raising, and program and economic development. Just before becoming the

University of North Texas's fourteenth president, she served as the interim chancellor of the North Carolina School of the Arts (NCSA). NCSA, the first state-supported residential school of its kind in the nation, has 1,200 students from eighth grade to post-master's programs in dance, design and production/visual arts, drama, filmmaking, and music. Success in this position prepared Bataille for her next opportunity—the University of North Texas (UNT), which houses one of the top music schools in the country.

Described as energetic, engaging, experienced, and enthusiastic, she was unanimously selected as the sole finalist in a nationwide presidential search. In 2006, Gretchen became the 116-year-old university's first female president. UNT is a research institution with roughly 34,000 students (12% African American and 11% Hispanic) enrolled in more than 200 undergraduate and graduate degree programs and has a budget of over $500 million. Her first priority was to get everyone moving in the same direction. "You have to learn about and cope with an institution and its culture. On a superficial level, when I came here, I was told I needed to understand that football is more important than basketball [it's the other way around in North Carolina] and that barbecue is beef and not chopped pork with vinegar. Then there's the bigger culture—the culture of the institution, and there are some parts of the culture in need of development at every university.

"When I went to North Carolina, I was told, 'The South is a place, the north is a direction.' It's true. Allegiances and history are strong, and there is a sense of continuing to do things 'the way they have always been done.' After being given that answer too many times, I ordered fifty buttons that said, 'Because we've always done it that way.' I gave them out whenever I got that answer and then asked the question again. [Texas is part of *The South.*] I need to order more now that I'm at UNT!"

One of her initial moves at UNT was to invite teams of national experts to conduct peer reviews in five areas: academic affairs, research, information technology, student development, and advancement operations. These groups examined both policies and structure and made recommendations that included restructuring academic support and administration, revamping hiring policies and procedures, dealing proactively with student access and retention, promoting and rewarding interdisciplinary research, and securing more outside funding.

"We certainly need to address access. Increasingly, those groups that don't go to college fail to do so because of economics. They're Black and poor, Hispanic and poor, White and poor, and the thing they have in common is they're poor. Most students now know race will not keep them out of college, but money will. In Texas, the unacceptable reality is that only 13 of 100 ninth graders will receive a college degree within six years after high school."

At UNT, "we've initiated two new scholarship funds—the Emerald Eagle Scholars and the Dr. Phil and Robin McGraw Scholarship Fund—to begin addressing access and retention issues." The Emerald Eagle program provides funding, mentoring, and tutoring for talented undergraduates with financial need. The McGraw Fund benefits graduates of Happy Hill Farm, a residential facility for at-risk students, many of whom have been victims of abuse and neglect. "When we announced this scholarship, a young girl who's been at Happy Hill for four years said to me, 'I want to be the first recipient of this scholarship and come to UNT.' When you see this beautiful young woman saying, 'This is me,' you realize the impact programs like these can have.

"We also need to think about the research profile of this campus, to ramp up our productivity, not just in terms of research dollars, but [also] in aspects that further the knowledge base of the world as well, whether it's in English, history, chemistry, biology, or the arts. Academics in general are entrenched in the way they go about their business. They tend to do only what they get credit for. They forget to just share. We need to reward people who exhibit stewardship for the broader institution and who serve as leaders and catalysts for change. If we want more interdisciplinary grant proposals, for instance, then we must have mechanisms in place that reward the effort it takes to write such proposals. The problem is, we say we want one thing, but we reward something different."

In their most recent book, *Faculty Career Paths*, Bataille and her former colleague, Betsy Brown, emphasize the growing presence of dual-career couples. At UNT, like many other places, misinterpreted nepotism policies and unenlightened thinking often hamper hiring practices and discourage good candidates from applying or staying if hired. "When I was at North Carolina, a member of the faculty at Chapel Hill came to visit me. She started talking about policies; I didn't know where she was going, but I said, 'I've been really upset by what I've seen here in terms of a lack of policies for partner accommodation.' She replied, 'You think we should have a spousal accommodation policy?' My rejoinder was, 'I'm not talking about spousal accommodation, I'm talking about being inclusive. We need to recognize that people coming here are in relationships.' And I'm thinking, oh, she's going to be really upset with me. But all of a sudden she just relaxes and says, 'You know, I'm gay, and I can't believe you actually believe that.' And why wouldn't I? It's the right thing to do. At the time, others on campus were not particularly accepting of this particular type of diversity. It boggles my mind. I can't understand an institution of higher education being so close-minded and judgmental.

"At UNT we must ensure that we hire faculty for the future, not the past. Some of our policies and procedures look like they have been around for years. Changing policy can be relatively easy compared to changing practice; old habits die hard. Nevertheless, we need to find ways to help UNT keep young faculty in Denton."

Perhaps the biggest hurdle facing UNT is fund-raising. The university's endowment is less than $100 million, which is relatively small for an institution of its size and age. Its regional distinction lingers, and its involvement in the area's economic development has been sporadic at best. In general, UNT flies low on almost everybody's radar screen.

"When I got the call from the chancellor and he said, 'I'm at the University of North Texas,' I said, 'Where's that?' He said, 'Denton, Texas,' and I said, 'Where's that?' We have to become better known. We're thought of as regional, but we're not. We have the best music program in the country. Musicians know about us; I want other people to know about us, too. Not knowing who we are hinders both fund-raising and our ability to stimulate economic development in the Denton-Dallas-Fort Worth area. Improving the situation will take time."

Out of necessity, however, Bataille's "longer view" at UNT is fairly short. "We're starting the quiet phase of a five-year campaign, but I have a three-year contract because, in the Texas higher education system, you can't have more than a three-year contract. It's somewhat problematic. What happens in three years if they decide they want a different president? I'm not concerned about me. I'm concerned about the institution because when you start building momentum toward fund-raising, people need to feel the president will be there for the long haul. Right now, I'm already at the end of my first year."

In anticipation of the campaign and to help raise the university's visibility, she recently completed UNT's first national alumni tour. "You fly to a city, arrive at three in the afternoon, go to a reception by 5:30, move on to a dinner by seven, fly out at seven the next morning. While you are there, you give speeches, talk to a zillion people in one evening, and ensure that every single one of them knows he or she is important to UNT. These are not easy tasks for many people. I think I have the right skills—I'm a pretty good communicator, I'm passionate about UNT, and I'm competent, but it's exhausting."

In general, the presidency takes a great deal of both physical and emotional stamina. Bataille contends that there are individuals who are smart enough to be college presidents but don't have the necessary physical energy. And, emotionally, some cannot differentiate among types of crises. "You have to learn to distance yourself from the crises that don't affect human beings. And you get very engaged in those that do. For instance, I don't worry about parking—that's just doing business. But, I will reflect on the impact of the shootings at Virginia Tech. It is a president's worst nightmare to think that her students have been killed and to realize that she couldn't do anything about it. If you cannot distinguish among types of crises, you burn out, first emotionally and then physically."

The energy required for the presidency derives, in part, from commitment. "If you're not passionate about where you are, then you shouldn't be there. You and the people around you have to feel totally engaged—that's absolutely, incredibly important. We have to believe that what we do is going to make a difference. Commitment in a competent person who can communicate effectively breeds credibility. Competence is almost too mild a word. It's not about putting one foot in front of the other; it's about being intelligent, having the mental capacity to get the job done, and doing the right thing. It's being ethical and having integrity and trusting that those who work for and with you are committed, competent, and honorable."

In the mid-1970s, Gretchen chaired the Iowa Civil Rights Commission. At the time, Iowa was the only state with a high school system in which its girls played six-girl basketball. The thought was that girls might not have the physical stamina to play five-girl ball. In fact, in some camps, the view still lingered that such activity would damage a girl's reproductive system. The problem for Iowa girls was that they couldn't compete for college athletic scholarships. Gretchen and other commissioners decided to take a stand on the issue and worked to have the rules changed, arguing the system violated Title IX. "I knew when that happened, it was the end of my being on the Civil Rights Commission. But I had to have integrity." Years later, an assistant basketball coach at Washington State University in Pullman wanted to know if Bataille was "the Gretchen Bataille from Iowa." The coach, who was from an Iowa family, went to college only because she earned a scholarship to play five-girl basketball. "It meant a lot to know that we had made a difference."

Making a difference means making decisions. "As a president you must be able to work with scholars, think clearly, organize well, weigh consequences, know your audience, and make decisions. Choosing not to decide perpetuates the status quo. To be honest, I've made decisions that in hindsight weren't the best, but I don't think I've ever made a decision that couldn't be reversed, or changed, or modified.

"Today, a president's discipline means less than his or her ability to understand the issues and deal with the unexpected. The day I received a phone call from risk management at 4:45

p.m., just about the time I get around to answering e-mail and going through the day's mail, provides a great example of the unexpected issues that can confront administrators. A student on an anthropology field trip to Belize was suing the university because he became ill after inhaling dry bat guano in a cave. All I could do was laugh, not because a student was ill but because this situation is not something any of us in leadership positions have been trained to resolve." (Bataille attended both the Harvard and the University of California management development programs. Neither covered bat guano.)

She has dealt with mud slides and lead contamination, learning about "100-year floods" in California (that happen much more frequently) and Environmental Protection Agency requirements. "Anything that can happen in a community can happen on a university campus because universities are like small cities. There are always going to be members of our community who think they are above the law or that policies are made for someone else. It's my job to ensure that institutional values are upheld, that those faculty or staff who choose to enrich themselves with state or student resources are held accountable. Unfortunately, I have been faced with having to request audits and then acting on them. I came to my position at the NCSA soon after an audit there resulted in several resignations, and at two other institutions, the necessity of ensuring fiscal integrity resulted in painful decisions about valued faculty and staff. What is critical is to realize that faculty and administrators are role models for our students as well as protectors of the state's resources."

Like others in similar positions, Bataille concedes that the amount of work can be overwhelming. "I would love to have a life," she laughingly admits. "It's one of the challenges for any single person in a leadership capacity—but more so for women because it's assumed that I can clean my house so I can host university guests and cook for and entertain them. In effect, I can run the household and do the work that needs to be done for the presidency, whereas men often get more help. I'm not going to ask my staff to pick up my cleaning or to do those kinds of household tasks. The challenge is doing both the job and the domestic duties.

"There are other kinds of challenges as well. When I was chancellor at the NCSA, the chancellor's house was in a not-so-good neighborhood. I came home alone late night after night. Three women were robbed at gunpoint in that neighborhood within about a two-week period. Thank goodness for the police. They patrolled my house; they were available. If I came home late they dropped by to be sure I was okay. Men usually don't worry about stuff like that.

"And to my mind, there's still a glass ceiling. In my first job, I made less than men and thought it was okay because I was a woman. I didn't like it, but I didn't have much choice. Since that time, we've seen incredible changes, but at the end of the day women still have a long way to go. There are still functions that are perceived as male, like leadership. When people ask me, How does it feel to be a woman president? How does it feel to be the first woman president? my response is that I think the Board of Regents decided it wanted to find the best person for the job, and I happened to be the one the board chose. I'm quite sure they didn't go out specifically looking for a woman.

"I've heard that some boards will not hire a woman unless she has a spouse. Why? What is having a spouse supposed to add? Is he a cook? For others, being single is problematic. I pretty much don't have anybody with me at any event because it's just easier that way." She did make an exception for her inaugural ball; her six- and nine-year-old grandsons, Justin and Austin, escorted her.

Although pragmatic about the realities of being a woman who happens to be a university president, she is also optimistic. "I am proud to be the leader for this time, but I recognize I am only temporary. It's about fit. Institutions need different kinds of presidents at different times. In every job I've had, I can honestly say I made a difference. Here, I will add my ideas and my contributions to those who came before me. We didn't get to where we are today by accident. We got here because a lot of great people believe in UNT. Each former president had a vision for UNT that moved the university forward; I hope to do the same. I hope my legacy is that we have a better university than we had when I came. It doesn't mean UNT was bad. It just means I will have done my job.

"In the end, I think working at a university is one of the most satisfying jobs in the world. We have great responsibilities, but also enormous opportunities. It is incumbent upon us to be the role models for the next generation, and to do it with integrity, with our values intact, and within an ethical framework."

BIBLIOGRAPHICAL NOTES

Gretchen M. Bataille's story is the culmination of interview transcripts; vitae; speeches, including her inaugural address; internal, official University of North Texas news releases; University of North Texas websites; newspaper articles from the *Denton Record-Chronicle* by reporters Leslie Wimmer, Monty Miller, Matthew Zabel, and Mandi Wallis; and Kelley Reese and Ellen Rossetti's "Beyond North Texas" (Fall 2006), *The North Texan*, 12–13.

THREE

HAVING FUN

Barbara Douglass
Northwestern Connecticut Community College

Aₗₜₕₒᵤ — ALTHOUGH PRAISE is always a hallmark of inaugural events, a local reporter noted that it flowed most profusely and genuinely at the 2005 inauguration of Northwestern Connecticut Community College's (NCCC) fifth president, Barbara Douglass. "She's the kind of leader the institution deserves, and her enthusiasm is literally palpable," commented Connecticut Senator Andrew Roraback. Her former employer, Conrad Mallett, president emeritus of Capital Community College, Hartford, Connecticut, praised her, saying, "Dr. Douglass has an entirely winning sense of humor, yet she takes everybody seriously, except herself. She is a wonderful human being who brings grace, honor, and distinction to the presidency of Northwestern Connecticut Community College." Shortly after her arrival, an area business owner remarked, "You can read a false face. She's genuine." NCCC students describe her as "easy to talk to," "friendly," "cool." The student senate president added, "She takes an active role in students' lives, an admirable quality in a president."

In a heartfelt, acceptance speech Douglass shared her beliefs on leadership. "As Benjamin Mays once said, 'The tragedy in life does not lie in not reaching your goal. The tragedy is having no goal to reach. Not failure but aiming low is the sin.'" She went on to say, "When I first arrived, I promised that I would not always agree with you or you with me. More often than not, we have agreed, but when we have not, we have disagreed with civility and with an eye toward compromise and always with a commitment toward what is best for our students. I promise to lead not only with intellect and hard work but with emotional intelligence and caring; not just to manage but to mentor. As fortunate as the college believes it is to have me, I'm just as fortunate or more so to have the college. My NCCC family has already challenged my intellect, spoken to my soul, and touched my heart." She heaped praise on her colleagues, mentors, supporters, and staff and joked, "There was more expert preparation for this inauguration than either of my two weddings—and, I expect, with a better outcome."

"Welcome to Northwestern Connecticut Community College, the small college that does great things," is the tagline Barbara has coined for the college. NCCC is the smallest of Connecticut's twelve community colleges with an enrollment of about 1,500 students. Founded privately in 1965 in a rural part of the state by a local group, it joined the Connecticut Community College System later that year. NCCC's average student age is twenty-eight, about two-thirds of its students are female, and almost all (90%) are White. Many are the first in their families to attend college, and most of them are preparing to transfer to a four-year degree program or for careers. The college boasts several unique programs, including Connecticut's only veterinary technology and American Sign language/interpreter preparation programs.

Douglass identifies closely with the challenges her students face. "I came from a lower-working-class family; my parents didn't go to college. My grandparents didn't get out of high school. If you're not expected to go to college, you're not encouraged to go to college. Not because your parents don't want you to be successful, but because they don't know anything about it. I'm sure my parents, if they were alive, would be thrilled that I'm a college president. They'd also be terribly surprised."

So, too, would her first speech professor. "In my first semester in college, I had to take public speaking. I had a very strong Boston accent. My first grade in college on the speech I gave in that class was an F. The instructor told me I was not college material, and I just wasn't going to make it. I'd love to find that person now."

Barbara overcame her rough start and earned a B.A. in English and politics from the University of Massachusetts, Boston. In 1973, at the age of twenty-two, she joined the Peace Corps. "It was a practical decision. I earned my teaching credentials at one of the few times in the history of this country that there was a teacher surplus. I couldn't find a job, but the Peace Corps fascinated me. You know, 'Join the Peace Corps, see the world,' and get some teaching experience."

She was assigned to teach English and humanities in Zaire in a rural girls' school run by Belgian nuns. On her way to Zaire she was involved in an international incident. "We were flying on East Africa Airways from London. Our plane refueled at Entebbe [Uganda]. We took off, but after a few minutes, the captain told us the flight had been ordered back to Entebbe by Uganda president General Idi Amin, because he found out there were Peace Corps volunteers on board. He sent MIGs to 'escort' us. Soldiers surrounded our plane and went through our luggage. We spent two days under armed guard in the airport. The third day they took us to a hotel where we had the opportunity to shower and clean up before they finally let us go on our way. No one was hurt. It was all very bizarre. It was in the time before plane hijacking, hostage-taking, and terrorism, and I didn't have the good sense to be scared.[1]

"Peace Corps assignments are usually for two years, but I had to cut my time short because my dad had what turned out to be a fatal stroke while I was in Zaire. Even though I was there for less than a year, I consider it to be a formative experience in my adult life."

She was paired with volunteer Sue Schommer, now a surgeon in California and still a close friend. They lived in a house without electricity or running water. "The experience instilled in me a love of other cultures, languages, and people and an appreciation for their desire to better themselves. It also made it terribly clear to me that we as Americans, as Westerners, have so much and take so much for granted, especially in terms of health and everyday needs, like nutrition. As I look at our culture, I am disturbed by our gross materialism. What the Peace Corps taught me is how little you need to get by and be happy.

"I began my community college career over thirty years ago. I saw how community colleges transformed lives. When I was in San Diego in the mid-1970s, the San Diego Community College District (SDCCD) was looking for ESL [English as a Second Language] teachers. That set my path. I started teaching in an adult

---

[1] The *New York Times* report of the incident indicated that the Peace Corps volunteers were being held at the personal order of General Amin, who asked that officials from East Africa Airways, Zaire, Rwanda, Burundi, or Somalia vouch for the identity of the volunteers. Just a few months before this incident, the U.S. ambassador, as well as 114 Peace Corps volunteers, had been withdrawn from Uganda because of unrest and violence. Zaire's President Mobutu

basic education high school preparation program. I worked with people whom I knew had great potential. They weren't dealt the best hand in life, but they were willing to work to become educated so they could make their lives better. I've been in community colleges ever since, and I've never wanted to be anywhere else. I finally realized my bliss by becoming a community college president. Every day, when I go to work, I smile when I see my campus. It's very much the cornerstone of my life now. To do what we do as presidents and CEOs, we have to have a passion not just for leadership, but, in my case, for community colleges. Leaders who lack passion are asleep at the wheel. They just want to keep the lid on things and keep the status quo.

"I was at a leadership academy a few weeks ago, and I was really disappointed. There was a panel of presidents, some new, others veteran. And all but one said, 'I've never taken a week off.' One had worked eighteen years and had never taken a week off. That is unhealthy.

"They talked about how they're never without their cell phones or BlackBerrys. One said he worked eighteen hours a day. I'm like, 'Come on, get a life.' You can't be effective that way. You might be putting in long hours and 'working hard,' but you're not working smart. I think that sends the wrong message to people. My colleague and mentor, Cathryn Addy, president of Tunxis Community College in Farmington, Connecticut, was the last one on the panel to speak. She said, 'I'm not a workaholic. I have a place in the Berkshires, where I go every other weekend. And I do my job. I'm committed to my students and my faculty and staff. You don't have to kill yourself.' All of the presidents on the

---

Sese Seko sent General Amin a telegram, which evidently led to the hostages' release. The famous Israeli raid on Entebbe occurred a few years later.

panel had passion for what they did. I liked them all, but in my mind, she was the most effective president there. What's best for your students and for the college is what matters.

"I don't think you inspire confidence by being a whirling dervish and having your car parked in your space every Saturday afternoon and Sunday night. You need to know your own limitations. I prioritize things. I get to work fairly early because I'm better in the morning. Some days I'm done at four. I'm tired and I want to go home and take a walk or go to Curves. So I just do it. I can't be effective any other way."

She also takes extended time to relax. She likes to unwind at her vacation home in St. Augustine, Florida. "People ask, 'What do you do in St. Augustine?' I say, 'Anything I want. Take a walk on the beach, go to a bookstore, or visit an art gallery.'" At home in Connecticut she enjoys nature, reads, goes tubing on the river near her house. "I like to think of myself as a woman of simple pleasures.

"There were young, fresh-faced division directors at the academy I just mentioned who might want to be presidents in the next ten years. If I were one of them and listened to those panelists, I'd never want to be a president! I tell presidential wannabes what a great time I have, and how much fun I have—like when we organized our first fund-raising gala, or how I was climbing around on our new building in a hard hat the other day. Or going to Rotary to share community college success stories. It's fun! One time, when the chancellor was signing my renewal contract giving me a raise, I told him, 'I can't believe you *pay* me to do this job.' We shouldn't portray the job as if it's all tedium. If it were, most of us wouldn't do it."

Barbara uses her time on campus to connect with her staff and employees and to take the pulse of the college. "The previous president was more of an external president. My habit is to show up between 8:00 and 8:15 in the morning and leave whenever I get done at night, which is usually long after five. After I had been at NCCC a few months, a senior faculty member said to me, 'You know, it used to be the president, ah, she's never here. And now it's, oh, God, the president, she's always here.' He laughed, 'And we're glad you are here.' There was this feeling of not being tended to, cared for. I understood it was amazingly important for me, as the new president, to have a presence on campus. I obviously need to meet with Rotary Clubs and bank presidents, but people need to know they can come see me in my office, that I am here for them."

In taking the job at NCCC, Barbara also made a commitment to "be there" for the community of Winstead. "When I was interviewed for the presidency, I decided to live in town. Our contracts demand that we live in Connecticut, but we don't have to live within our college service area. I wanted to make the community my home, so I live four miles from campus. I believe that kind of involvement is essential for the president."

Many of Barbara's beliefs about how to lead NCCC are based on her understanding of its culture and the role that culture plays in shaping the manner in which she leads and changes the organization. "The culture of my college is one of well-deserved pride in its liberal arts transfer sequence and in its positive connection to the community. The college is a mainstay of the community. That connection is something we take advantage of. Thirty-three of the college's 100 full-time employees, faculty, and staff have degrees from our community college. I know a great deal about the college. I know all about its budget and its academic policies because I have worked in the Connecticut system before. Faculty and staff give me an appreciation of its history and culture. But I challenge them. I say, 'I need you to take that history and work toward the future with me. Because what we were doing in 1982 isn't going to work now.'"

Douglass has worked as a community college administrator in California, Florida, and Connecticut. Along the way she gained experience in continuing education, grant writing, academic leadership, and student affairs, as well as serving a short stint as acting president of Capital Community College in Hartford, Connecticut. "I've jumped around quite a bit. There's a part of me that greatly admires people who can stay put and stick with it. And I admire them even more when they don't become entrenched. I believe there is stability, and then there is entrenchment. A CEO is very wise to seek progress through stability, but entrenchment throws up all kinds of roadblocks.

"There is tenure for faculty here and strong faculty and staff unions. This gives employees stability, which is good, but it can also give them the sense that they never have to change what they are doing. Right now, I am trying to add a nursing program to our curriculum. There is a state and national nurse shortage and only five nursing programs in the twelve Connecticut community colleges. Seems like a no-brainer, but it's been a struggle every step of the way. Some faculty and staff resist the change over minor concerns, like more competition for parking or choice classroom space. With the support of key faculty and staff, I am taking huge risks raising money in the community and lobbying the legislature for funds while others remain hung up on such minor issues. I don't have much patience for that kind of thinking. I say, 'Get on the bus and help us change.' There are some people who never will get on the bus. Well, the bus is leaving without them. I don't reward obstructionist behavior.

"Risk taking is important as a safeguard against entrench-ment. An institution that doesn't change and doesn't grow is dying. As president, I have to guard against parochialism, a cer-tain we've-always-done-it-this-way attitude. It's not like I'm a hedge fund trader; I'm not taking those kinds of risks everyday. But, a president must bring in ideas that are essential to her own leadership style. It's a balance of respect for the history and traditions of the college and the community and the ability to bring a new perspective where necessary. Because I am at a col-lege that is so wonderful but can be very cautious, one of my messages is: try something new. Once a week. For example, devi-ate from your lesson plan in the classroom. Or have a talk with the admissions director about our incoming high school students or what we know about our college dropouts. Do something that will help make this college a better place. If it doesn't work out, that's okay. We have to have open minds, exploring what's best for our students.

"I set up what I call The Extra Mile Award. I found this old cross-country award with a runner on the top to use as a trophy for the person or group that has gone the extra mile to help our students or our campus. We have an all-college meeting at least every other month, and I present the award at that meeting. It is totally at my discretion; no nominations. It has absolutely no material value, except the recipient can have lunch with me if he or she wants to. I make this award a fun thing. The first group that got it were the Science Divas, three extraordinary female sci-ence faculty who do all the extras—like partnering with the high school and sponsoring the Ecology Club. They're smart, they're tough, and the students love them."

Her consistent respect for others, honesty, and authenticity provide the foundation of her credibility and her ability to be effective. "When you're the president, you have a *lot* of freedom. You can do just about anything. You have power and how you use it day-to-day speaks to your integrity and your ethics. It's so easy to misuse it. When I'm wrong, or when I've made a mistake, I own up to it. If I've overreacted, I apologize. If I am truly irritated with someone, I'll write out my thoughts. If I write something in anger, I wait to send it until the next day. And I'll edit it before I send it. If you show that you're in control of yourself and you can handle whatever's out there, people are going to have much more trust in and respect for you. I've seen presidents just tear into people in public and it's unseemly. I've told my people I will always reprimand in private and praise in public. I don't think there's anything uglier than a screaming match in the hallway.

"Recently, all of the faculty members were attending a presentation by our academic dean on learning outcomes and assessment during a campus professional development day. It's an important topic and an area in the last accreditation report where we needed to improve. The dean was doing a terrific job. I looked around the room and everyone was paying attention except one professor in the back. He was flipping papers, and it was obvious he was grading assignments. I thought, 'Okay, I need to respect this person's individuality, but this behavior is not acceptable; it's rude.' I didn't want to call him out like a fifth-grade classroom teacher. So I got up and walked around to where he was sitting near the door and I tapped on it. He looked up at me and I whispered, 'Are you grading papers?' He said, 'Well, yeah, I am. I already know about assessment. I don't need this.' I said, 'That doesn't cut it. That's not appropriate. The bottom line is it's disrespectful to Jean.' Well, he stopped, and a little later he actually moved to the front and participated. My actions sent a message to everyone in that room about how this president operates. You can be an individual, but you're not going to do it at the expense of the college or others.

"Sometimes great injustices can be done in the name of individuality. As the CEO, I have to be driven by what's best for the college and what is best for the students, not what is best for an individual. While I respect people's individuality, it can't drive the college. I believe I have to support the greatest good for the greatest number.

"That means, I must sometimes move into unfamiliar territory. I went from an academic dean position to vice president of instruction to president. I'm good at focusing on academic programs as I plan for the college's future. It's where I feel safest. But as president, I need to keep the institution running. It's like twirling different plates at the same time; you've got to pay attention to everything. For example, fund-raising has become very important because of changes in state appropriations. In 1992, when I got my Ph.D. at the University of Texas, Austin, in its community college leadership program, they didn't talk about fund-raising. I have no experience in it either, but I do have experience in communication and organization and laying out the steps needed to reach a goal. I'm out of my comfort zone, but I've got skills I can bring to this new arena. I can go out to the community and do what I call targeted schmoozing. I can use the new building we are finishing up as a springboard for future fund-raising for a new student center. It's a challenge, but it's a lot of fun, too. I'll keep at it because it supports the most important thing we do, which is to provide the best teaching and learning experiences for our students."

Doing so takes confidence. "I've been told that I am self-confident and self-assured. Even if I don't feel it on a particular day,

I act it. Some of it goes back to my history. I got to this point through hard work, taking risks, being smart, getting educated. Sometimes I still think to myself, this isn't bad for a working-class kid from Boston. That's the kind of self-confidence I have come to possess over the years. And it's the kind of self-confidence I want to instill in our students, especially our women students."

Douglass has given a great deal of thought to what women need to know about being effective leaders. "I'm 'femocentric.' It's important to let women who are coming along after us know what it takes. That you must, for instance, have finesse in communication. You've got to be at ease speaking in front of groups and conducting meetings. It's hard, but the more you do it, the better you get. You also have to listen. Being able to just sit and listen is more than half of communicating. It is the hardest thing we do. It's much more tiring than talking, but it keeps you from shooting from the hip. Being able to communicate with wit and a sense of humor, not sarcasm, always gives a leader an edge."

She has developed three maxims over the years that guide her and that she shares with other women who aspire to leadership positions. One, pace yourself. Making significant change takes time. Give others the time to become accustomed to your ideas. Two, choose your battles. You are in this for the long haul; be strategic with your influence and your energy. And, three, this is a job; it is not your life. Take your job seriously, but don't take yourself too seriously. "The job is an important part of my life, and it's a part of my life that makes me feel fulfilled, but it is not my life."

Personal losses have helped Barbara realize that work and job should be kept in perspective. At the time of her inauguration, her brother was unable to attend because he was battling cancer.

He lost that battle two months later. "That was a tough time. You never expect to outlive your younger brother. My entire family is deceased—father, mother, sister, brother." Like many single women, Barbara Douglass has created a surrogate family, a network of friends and mentors that spans the continent from Connecticut to Florida to California, people she visits whenever she can get away or needs renewal. "That's important. You can't go it alone."

She also believes that women need to know that "leadership is about more than your IQ. It's about having common sense and being able to set goals and build a team. It's about having the emotional intelligence that gives you the ability to connect with people, have them see the future the way you see it, and get them to work toward it. Those are skills that determine your success as a CEO. Being smart is certainly a plus. But you must also be fair, as objective as possible, and no-nonsense. I think that what harms presidents more than incompetence is arrogance, insensitivity, greed, and being brash. These are the bigger sins."

Twice divorced, Barbara acknowledges her inability to find the right match in marriage. Her first marriage to her undergraduate boyfriend was a form of escape. "It became very apparent to me that, when my father died, my mother expected me to stay in Boston and take care of her, even though she was forty-eight and in perfectly good health. It freaked me out. There are only two ways that a nice Italian or Irish American girl leaves her parents' house, either in a pine box or in a white dress. We got married because my mother believed the woman has to go with her husband." The marriage lasted seven years. "I think Charles and I valued different things. I felt it was important to do the right thing, and he felt it was important to win. It caused friction."

Barbara was single for eleven years before marrying again in 1992. By then, she had begun to build a career plan that included presidential aspirations. The couple moved from California to the East Coast to be closer to her husband's child from a former marriage. Barbara became the academic dean at Capital Community College in Hartford, Connecticut. "I was the big wage earner. He worked at a small, private high school making almost nothing. I was driving an hour each way every day because we lived in a community near his school. I was becoming quite ambitious by then. I had just finished my Ph.D. on a Kellogg fellowship. I think he was extremely threatened by my ability and ambition and, perhaps, my professional stature. He was immature. He wanted someone to bring home the big salary, but who would also cook and clean and not ask any questions. I said, 'No way. You get out of school at 2:30. You take care of the household chores.' It just did not work out. We divorced after four years. It's funny how things happen. I moved to Connecticut because of my husband's family ties, but the professional experiences and opportunities I gained there, in part, led me to the presidency at NCCC."

In the end, while the success of the marriage between Barbara Douglass and NCCC will depend on her effectiveness as a leader, it will also be due in no small measure to her outlook. She lives her life by her favorite Ben & Jerry's motto: "If it's not fun, why do it?" She leads by the words she uses to end every NCCC convocation ceremony: "Let's have fun. Let's get to work."

BIBLIOGRAPHICAL NOTES

The chapter on Barbara Douglass was based on multiple in-depth interviews, informal conversations, and her inaugural speech and vitae; the Northwestern Connecticut Community College website, catalogue, Office of Institutional Research Fact Book, and student newspaper; a newspaper article by Karsten Strauss in the *Register Citizen* (April 25, 2005); and several articles by George Krimsky in the *Republican-American* (April 2005).

FOUR

MOVING FORWARD

Mildred García
Berkeley College

M ILDRED (MILLIE TO MOST PEOPLE) GARCÍA had been on
the job exactly four days. "I was driving into Manhattan
on the George Washington Bridge to my New York City office
when the second plane hit the World Trade Center. All I could
think about was getting back to our main campus in the heart of
New York City. I had a campus full of students and staff. I pulled
the entire campus together in the lobby, telling everyone we had
each other. I asked them to pray to whomever they prayed to.
That campus is only two blocks from Grand Central Station.
There were multiple bomb scares every day, which meant evacu-
ating Grand Central. Hundreds of individuals would come out
into the street in front of our campus. Everyone was afraid, not
knowing what to expect. During those first months of my presidency, I focused on pulling the community together because it
was important that we had faith and felt hopeful, supported, and
a part of a caring community. It was a passionate time. It was a
very hard time. Nothing—no course, professor, or degree—
prepared me for it."

Rarely has a college president begun her tenure on the eve of such a defining moment. That day, Berkeley lost fourteen students and alumni, all of whom worked in the World Trade Center, and the husband of one of its faculty, who was on the flight from Pennsylvania.

Berkeley College, a for-profit institution, is made up of three New York City and four New Jersey campuses, all located within forty minutes of downtown New York City. In 2001, Millie became its first system-wide president. Before becoming president, she had served on its Board of Trustees for nine years. "I took a risk coming to Berkeley. I spoke to all my friends across the country and only one of them cautioned me against taking this job. But academics can be elitists. And for others, the perception exists that somehow I settled for less or wasn't quite competent enough to secure a presidency in a more traditional nonprofit institution. I believe, however, that fit is more important than other people's perceptions.

"I hadn't really thought about a presidency until ten years or so before coming here. But once I decided to look for one, I was persistent and followed my passion. My goal was to become president of an urban institution with Berkeley's profile—one that serves a diverse, first-generation student body, offering academically strong associate's and bachelor's degrees in a campus community committed to access and the success of every student who enrolls. I am fortunate to have realized my goal! Berkeley has the most diverse student body I have worked with in my entire career. It's a microcosm of what is happening in the United States.

"I am fiercely committed to the success of Berkeley and, more important, my students' success. You must be really committed to the organization, its mission, and, more important, to its people. It's not the building, it's the people who make up this organization. I'm passionate about this institution and I communicate well about it because of the students we serve. Passion and communication go hand in hand. If you're passionate about the organization, you understand its culture, you know what you're talking about, and you believe in what you say. When I speak about this institution, I can speak about the student body."

Berkeley's students and her passion for them and the institution drive Millie. Many are the first in their families to attend college, and one-third of them are Latino/Latina. Although 10% of them hail from countries other than the United States, the vast majority of Berkeley's 5,000 students grew up in the New York City metropolitan area. Over 90% of them receive federal, state, or institutional financial aid, and all have hopes and dreams of bettering themselves through education.

"I identify with my students because our early lives run parallel. I was born in Brooklyn. My parents and five eldest siblings had moved from Puerto Rico to New York City in 1946. There's eight years between my sister and me. Our parents didn't really expect my younger brother's and my arrival. We lived on Front Street. When I was twelve, my father passed away and we moved into the Farragut Public Housing Project. I was brought up in a neighborhood of mostly families of color who spoke both Spanish and English. Although my older brothers and sisters attended public schools in low SES [socio-economic status] neighborhoods, because of the times, I was fortunate enough to begin my education in an elementary school in the affluent neighborhood of Brooklyn Heights. Even so, one of the things that will stay with me forever is that some of us from the neighborhood made it; and some of us didn't.

"I can speak about our students' dreams, their hopes, their aspirations because they were mine. It's all about opportunity. It's about validating people and letting them know they have potential and they can succeed. Ours are students to whom most institutions have closed their doors. We're taking in smart students who need assistance, who need polishing. We listen carefully to them. Faculty, administrators, and staff pay attention to the silences of those students who seem to struggle. We seek them out. We try to find out what's going on in their lives. Do they like this institution? Is this the right match for them? We try to touch each student in a very personal way."

Berkeley works to meet the needs of both part- and full-time students. Two of its seven campuses offer residential facilities for more traditional students, but many working students attend one campus close to work during the week and another nearer home on the weekend. They can also enroll in online courses. Associate's degrees can be earned in as little as eighteen months and bachelor's degrees in three years. Of Berkeley's $75.5 million budget, over $14 million goes to qualified students in the form of grants and scholarships. The school also offers intensive tutoring and lifetime free career counseling, of which many of its 50,000 alumni still avail themselves. As Millie told one reporter, "By educating all Americans, we not only support families in achieving greater social and economic equality, we reinforce the strength of the economy in the United States and of this country as a world leader. We fail our students when they drop out and fade away.

"I'm passionate about these students because that's where I came from. That's my neighborhood. That's my story.

"My parents always said, 'The only inheritance a poor family can leave its children is a good education.' My mom (now also deceased) provided the model. One summer, when I was fourteen, I wanted to work with my cousin in a factory making pocketbooks and she let me. Best education she could have given me. The experience was so demeaning, I swore I'd never work in a factory again.

"Mom supported us on a factory worker's salary with help from us children who worked after school. Evenings, when I returned home from my job at May's department store, a home-cooked meal always sat warming on the radiator. When a high school counselor told me I'd set my sights too high, that I ought to think about becoming a secretary, I vowed to prove her wrong. I was the first in my family to attend college. Getting the doctorate was important for my family. It changed the way we see the world; it changed me. Today, our family (four living siblings; twenty-nine nieces, nephews, and grand nieces and nephews; and me) stresses the importance of college as soon as children are born!

"We are an extremely close family. We get together for holidays and we stay connected as much as possible. Twenty-five family members attended my inauguration at Berkeley. One of the first things I told Berkeley's board was that I understood why two or four tickets for graduation ceremonies just didn't work. Our students are like me; our extended families are our families.

"Some of my nieces and nephews are my contemporaries, so we are friends and share experiences. I am godmother to a niece and nephew and to four of my grand nieces and nephews. In the Latino tradition, godparents are extremely important—quite frankly like second parents, and although I don't have children, my godchildren and nieces and nephews are my children.

"In fact, one of my nephews, who is learning disabled, was having a real rough time in New York City. His life was going the route of many men of color who at times lose hope. At a critical point in his life, Damian came to live with me in Phoenix when I was at Arizona State. We surrounded him with positive young people his own age, connected him with learning disability professionals, had male professors mentor him, and found him a position as a computer technician. In his first college course, a web design course, he received his first B, and he realized he had potential and promise. Today he lives in Phoenix, is a computer technician for the Peoria School District, bought himself a home, and has turned his life around.

"College opened doors for me. It helped me find my calling. I attended New York City Community College, graduating with a degree in business. I then enrolled at Bernard M. Baruch College, where I earned a bachelor's degree in business administration. During this period of my academic career, I worked at retail outlets and as a secretary to help pay the bills. Later I taught business courses at La Guardia Community College while pursuing an M.B.A. at New York University. I earned a second master's and a doctorate, both in higher education administration, at Columbia University Teachers College, while working for Hostos University as the executive assistant to the president and later as the chief student affairs officer.

"When I graduated, I took an administrative position at Montclair State University in New Jersey, but continued to live in New York. Even though I was an administrator, I took time to teach a course every semester. I gradually worked my way into the position of assistant vice president for academic affairs. From Montclair, I moved to Arizona State University [ASU] as vice provost for academic personnel, professor in the Social and Behavioral Sciences Department, and associate director of the Hispanic Research Center.

"Each institution taught me something new. I was naïve enough to think that all institutional types are the same, and they're not. They all have different cultures. My work at LaGuardia helped me understand student academic development. I learned to put Ernest Boyer's 'teaching as scholarship' to work at Montclair State. And at ASU, I learned about research and gained an understanding of Washington, D.C., policies and politics. Along the way, I continually engaged in professional development activities. I participated in Harvard University's Seminar for New Presidents, the American Association of State Colleges and Universities' Millennium Leadership Institute, the Bryn Mawr Program for Women in Higher Education Administration, Harvard University's Institute for Educational Management, and Salzburg's Leadership Fellows program. If I'd stayed at one type of institution and not continued to educate myself, I wouldn't have gained the experience that helped me adapt to Berkeley's culture.

"Being a president here is not the same as being a president somewhere else. Effective leaders know you must understand the culture before you try to change it; that's definitely true for me here. Although I'm very familiar with the student body, the organization's culture was very different from Arizona State's, Montclair's, or CUNY's. The presidency at a research university is very different from one here, or at a community college, or a state college, or an HBCU [historically Black colleges and universities],

HIS [Hispanic-serving institutions], or tribal college. I needed to come in and listen and learn and understand the culture before I knew where we were going next. It's important because you find out where you are effective, where you are comfortable—where the right match for you is.

"This school's mission of preparing members of underrepresented groups (originally women only) for the business workplace hasn't varied over its seventy-five-year history. We ask businesses: What is it that we can do to make our students employable? Based on continual feedback, Berkeley designs programs of study that include liberal arts preparation, business training, high levels of computer literacy, and extensive internships. It works. Ninety-five percent of Berkeley graduates find employment related to their studies within ninety days after graduation.

"Berkeley can be a model for other colleges that serve large proportions of disadvantaged students. We are not, however, taken seriously because of the predisposition of other institutions to look at us as being 'less than' because we are a for-profit institution. Moving Berkeley into the limelight as a model for other institutions requires a shift in organizational culture on our part—a building of our academic credentials to complement our business acumen. Traditionally, Berkeley has been a two-year business school; now it offers four-year degrees. We've hired more people with Ph.D.s to balance the entrepreneurial emphasis of the organization with its academic profile. In doing so we've created a schism between old and new faculty and administrators. People who have worked here thirty, twenty-five, or even ten years are scared of change, afraid of being left out. We now must build a safe environment in which people with and without advanced degrees can interact with each other at work and in social settings, to learn together as a learning community. For example, every year we have an All Associates' Day where we bring in a keynote speaker (one year we brought Vincent Tinto[1]). We break up into groups to discuss how what the speaker said affects the areas where we work. At the end of the day, we dance, play games, and get to know each other.

"We have also changed the way cabinet-level administrators think and work. I began assigning readings from both business and higher education to broaden our perspective. I make sure to read the *New York Times, Harvard Business Review,* and the *Chronicle of Higher Education.* It's critical. We talk about the issues and think through where we are and where we want to go. Today we think differently. I ask each vice president to engage in professional development. It's good for them and it's good for the institution. I ask them to write a yearly reflective piece, to think about the year, about where they're going, about whether they are making progress. We started a staff development program in an effort to move the organization forward. Upper-level administrators identify individuals for the program who demonstrate leadership potential. Staff members (around ten at a time) participate in activities designed to fine-tune their leadership abilities and provide them with an opportunity to determine whether they want to pursue administrative positions in the future.

"I firmly believe that you bring in, or raise up, the best people you can, strong people, and you listen to them. I look for people who complement my strengths and compensate for my weak areas. For instance, I know very clearly that I have the right provost. We're both academics, but I'm the big-picture person who

---

1 Vincent Tinto is a highly regarded scholar who studies college-age students.

loves to communicate big ideas. I love to speak in public. He calls me the social butterfly. He loves detail work—to be alone in an office writing reports. If I had hired a provost like me, we wouldn't get the work done.

"We've just started a strategic planning process. It took me three years to convince my board that we need to do that. Before now, planning meant putting together a wish list and at the end of the year checking: Did we make it or not? If we didn't 'make it,' 'it' stayed on the wish list for the following year. With strategic planning, we set goals and targets and we measure our outcomes. We have a clearer picture of our future and we use institutional research much more effectively than before. We make sure we know what our market is and what our retention rate is. Every division now thinks about enrollment management, not only within units but across them as well. I had one vice president who told a board member at a social event that our enrollment management process was useless. I called him in and said, 'I respect and value your judgment and your opinion. But don't tell us in committee meetings that this is the best process you've ever been involved in, and then go to a board member the very next week and tell him it is a waste of time. Which one is it? You can disagree with me, but you have to be truthful. If you can't, then you can't be on this team.'

"I share power. I don't have a problem with someone else representing me in the community or the provost making the decisions in my absence. That's why you hire people. 'If you need me to do everything, then why do I need you?' I don't know if the leadership team perceives me as powerful, but they all see me as honest. And honesty is the basis of trust. It's extremely important that they know that I'm a straight shooter, that they can trust me.

"The board sees me as powerful. The board sees me as credible. In fact, one board member said to me, 'Your being here has brought this institution instant credibility.' Why? Because I've done research, I speak publicly, I publish books, I'm accepted by the higher education community." She also garners respect from the larger community. "There are so few Latinas in high places that once they discover you, you are asked to serve on every committee." Almost immediately after García started her new job, New York City and the states of New York and New Jersey asked her to be on boards and commissions, such as serving on New York City's Workforce Improvement Board and co-chairing a commission on education in New Jersey.

"Once I said yes to board positions, all I could think of was, not only do I have to deliver, I have to deliver on time, and it has to be superior work. For women and people of color, your first shot out is what they will remember. It's the only shot you have. One mistake and they'll never ask again. The majority of men can do something terrible at an institution, and a month later or six months later, they'll have another presidency. Women and people of color don't have that luxury.

"The baseline is confidence. I think that's particularly true for women and people of color. The only thing that hampers success is the self-imposed, self-defeating fear of failure—that overwhelming doubt that you can achieve your goals. Confidence is relative when you speak about confident people who are different. They lie outside the norm. In my experience, although we in higher education say we want diversity and we want women, what we really mean is we want diversity and we want women who are like us (meaning they espouse traditional models of leadership). Fall into this mold and you can join the club. We tend to look for someone who looks and acts like the ones who served before. People really want a cookie cutter way of choosing leaders, and it's not that easy. I've brought in new people here and their first years here have been hell because they were different.

"For women and men of color, confidence is not enough; opportunity must exist. I think there are a lot of opportunities out there, but the barriers are high. There is a backlash against powerful, assertive women. Look at how many women have been asked to step down or who have stepped down voluntarily, knowing that controversy was ballooning. Where are they today? They just don't come back.

"It's so much harder for women. We are always under a microscope. If you are strong, you're seen as bitchy. Men, in contrast, are seen as assertive; they know what they're doing. They're leaders who tend to be Lone Rangers and make all the decisions. Women who are more collaborative, which I am, appear to be too touchy-feely. Increasingly, men are taking this more collaborative tact and, as they do, it will be thought of more consistently as a way to lead.

"If you're single, it's very difficult. They're always watching whom you go out with, who calls you, what you do, what you wear. Men can get away with four suits, one navy blue, one black, one brown, and another gray. We wear the same outfit in the same month and they're talking about it.

"I am often asked if I am single by choice. I am single because I haven't met the right match for me. Being a president and being single is very complex. Singles don't have a spouse helping with the social events, planning the meals, helping to fund raise, running errands, and paying the bills. Everything falls on the shoulders of the single president. Your calendar can get out of control because no one is at home expecting you. You tend to stay at work later, pack your calendar, and go out or travel without limits. You need to become your own conscience. I guess the only thing that makes it easier when you're single is that you are not juggling two lives."

She further points to a more insidious problem. "We don't talk about it in higher education, but women can be hard on women. Women have been socialized either not to want other women to be their bosses or to want or need to be queen bees. Or they simply do not want anyone of color as a boss, which is something else we don't talk about publicly. My strongest opponents when I've gone for interviews have been women. It's quite disheartening. I don't know whether we'll ever break that barrier."

Confidence and opportunity are only part of the story. In addition, she says, "You always have to be on top of the game. You must be competent. There's always a higher hurdle for women and people of color. And in higher education you must follow the perceived correct path to leadership. If you want to be a president, especially if you are a woman or person of color, you need to be a faculty member—to teach, publish, and attain tenure. And you always have to think about how to demonstrate the level of competence expected. Every time you try for a new position, it brings you back to thinking about competence. It's either you haven't taught enough or you haven't written enough, you've written in the wrong area, or you have the wrong degree. That's why competence has always been and will remain important to me. Not because I don't believe I'm competent, but because women and people of color have to be 200% better for others to see them as competent.

"Competent or not, it's risky. I don't think people understand the uncertainty of the presidency. I definitely do. I know that I am eight votes away from unemployment. These jobs are not forever. Every institution needs different presidents with different skill sets at different times. At the end of my contract, we'll see if I'm still the right person for the position. It will depend on what the board feels and what the community feels and how I feel. These jobs eat up your time.

"I came in running a short sprint and ran it for my first two years before I understood this is a marathon. I came here trying to do everything all at once—being available 24/7. I realized that's not good, so I started to pull back a little bit. To be effective, I have to carve out that time for myself—to reflect, reenergize, and refresh. I meditate, pray, and have faith in God. I am a spiritual person; that's what keeps me grounded, hopeful, and excited about life and all its possibilities. In addition, I began dancing again. I love to dance, especially salsa and Latin dances, and I enrolled in a yoga class. I try to eat healthy, which is extremely difficult because of all the eating out that you do as president. I also began traveling for fun. My cousin and I have traveled to Barcelona and London together. Although I have traveled alone, I find I don't enjoy it as much as traveling with family or close friends. You can't share the sites, the cultural experiences, and the fabulous meals if you are alone." And she engages in personal capacity building. "I am an active member of the American Council on Education and get support from a cadre of advisors comprised of other presidents and confidants, from both in and outside higher education. If you go it alone and can trust no one, you burn out. I've known a couple of presidents, one a woman and one a man of color, who never sought help, pretended all was well when it wasn't, got into trouble, became insular, and are no longer presidents. We are not perfect, and I think people feel that if they ask for advice or talk about a problem, they'll be seen as weak.

"I have been blessed with so many mentors along the way. From my doctoral advisor at Columbia, to presidents and faculty I've met at national organizations, to contemporary colleagues who supported me through the dissertation and are still my confidants today. These individuals are available to talk through the issues, provide advice, and even tell me when I am traveling too much. But in general, women don't network enough, and it is crucial to individual survival and success. Women in powerful positions need to mentor those who aspire to leadership. We need to find more ways of supporting each other. I mean specifically nationally based, formalized programs for young women who want to be administrators or faculty members—where young women talk about their hopes, dreams, and aspirations, and seasoned women lead them in the right direction through mentoring—moving them forward. I know I don't do enough personally to help bring up the newer generation."

In August 2007, Millie moved west again and took over the presidency at California State University, Dominguez Hills (CSUDH). "Leaving Berkeley was a difficult decision for me. I had been nominated for the Dominguez Hills position. My board at Berkeley had unanimously reappointed me to a second term. We had reached great goals, and I was at the top of my presidency. Yet, here was another one of those opportunities that was the right match for me—an urban public university, which *U.S. News and World Report* called the most diverse university west of the Mississippi. Could I head a public university with the type of students I am committed to and create the learning environment with the accountability and outcomes I was fortunate to be a part of at Berkeley?"

CSUDH is larger than Berkeley College, and its student population is extremely diverse, 40% Hispanic, about 31% African American, 18% White, 11% Asian, and less than 1% American Indian. Immigrant and visa students on the campus represent ninety-three countries. Programs include both baccalaureate and master's-level degree options and the opportunity to begin the Ed.D. in educational leadership coming in 2009. "It was a wonderful challenge, and while leaving New York City—my home— was difficult, I feel I can always go back. I've heard so many times that it is better to leave when you are on top, and for me at Berkeley, that was certainly the case. I truly believe you should not overstay your welcome, and I believed my administration had made its mark and Berkeley could move to another level under another president."

Moving forward is key to Millie—whether she's the one doing the moving or she's helping Berkeley or Dominguez Hills tap into unrealized potential. As she so aptly puts it, "People don't rise to low expectations." So she keeps hers high, and her "in a New York minute," can-do spirit clearly goes a long way toward helping her succeed. In 2007, *Hispanic Business* named Millie one of the hundred most influential Hispanics in America.

BIBLIOGRAPHICAL NOTES

Mildred García's story represents the synthesis of multiple data sources. Included in these are interview transcripts; vitae; Berkeley College websites; and the following newspaper articles: Rev.

Willie J. Smith, "Success Is Possible for All Who Believe," *The Times* (August 4, 2002); Alison Bert, "García Takes Up Reins at Berkeley," *The Journal News* (April 24, 2002); Elizabeth Hlotyak, "Westchester Meets New Berkeley College President," *Westchester Business Journal* (November 19, 2001); Tom Boud, "Berkeley College Welcomes New Pres," *Dateline Journal* (January 3, 2002); and Frances Ann Kosa, "70 Years of Change But Still 1 Mission," *The Star-Ledger* (February 2002). Other resources include *The Berkeley Focus* (Fall 2006); "Mujeres of Distinction," *Hispanic Outlook* (February 23, 2004); Stephen Burd, "For-Profit Colleges Want a Little Respect," *The Chronicle of Higher Education* (September 5, 2003, A23–26,); Irene Lumpkin, "Profile of a Leader in Education, Dr. Mildred García," *Garden State Woman*, 48 (2007); and the California State University Dominguez Hills website.

FIVE

STILL STANDING

Carol C. Harter
University of Nevada, Las Vegas

I N HINDSIGHT, excerpts from the 1994 advertisement for University of Nevada, Las Vegas's (UNLV) presidency underscore the ironic situation in which Carol Harter, as the university's first woman president, found herself. The position posting noted, "A new metropolis—without long traditions of respect for higher education—has difficulty comprehending its evolving university. Recent [bad] publicity has made external leadership challenging. Throughout the community can be found anxiety, skepticism, loss of trust, disappointment, frustration, anger, and a readiness to fix blame—all from people who hope deeply for the university's success."

The posting went on to say, "honesty, integrity, openness, fairness, and a commitment to academic values" were basic requirements in UNLV's next president as he or she sought to improve the university's image, both on and off campus. It further stated, the "president will have the toughness and inner strength to remain focused on larger, more important, institutional issues in the midst of a sometimes adversarial climate." It ended by suggesting that UNLV sought an opportunity-oriented president who would be motivated by the "appeal of fashioning a great national university from excellent raw materials."

In Carol Harter, UNLV got exactly what it asked for. During her presidency she articulated a vision that changed the mission of the institution and engaged the entire campus in an extensive planning process in which faculty, staff, and administrators set goals and revamped reward systems that reinforced the new vision and redefined the university. Carol pushed and pulled UNLV where it would not have gone on its own—from its comfortable station as "Tumbleweed Tech" to research university. She created a legacy most would envy and did it in an environment many would not care to tackle. In doing so she gained the respect of many but never totally dissuaded her naysayers.

In UNLV, Carol got a bit more than she anticipated. Harter spent most of her academic career in New York and Ohio, where her hard-hitting, straightforward, no-nonsense approach to leadership served her well. She spent nineteen years at Ohio University, beginning her career in 1970 on the English department faculty. She entered administration by happenstance when all untenured faculty received pink slips because of massive budget cuts. She was nominated for and accepted the ombudsman position, as she put it, "armed only with tenacity and the power of persuasion." After two years she was appointed vice president and dean of students, a position she held for six years before the president redirected her to the vice presidency of administration. Over the course of seven years in this role, she learned about facilities management, fiscal affairs, and labor relations. Her first presidency followed. When she took over the State University of New York at Geneseo in 1989, she inherited an institution suffering from across-the-board budget cuts brought on by a governor who did not support public higher education. After six years, she wanted to go where she could build a school. Her choice: the University of Nevada, Las Vegas.

As the first woman to hold each of her first four administrative positions, she learned about leadership "inside" the academic culture. To her, "knowing who faculty are as human beings, what they care about, and why" undergirds the role of administration in the academy. "Basically, we're here to protect faculty so they can think, reflect, work with students, and do research. My experience [prior to her arrival at UNLV] told me that the outside community agreed with this assessment.

"Coming out of a more progressive East Coast environment, I made certain assumptions that I shouldn't have made. As a result, I had to make a lot of changes in terms of how I approached issues that surround building a young university. For UNLV, I believed that the question was, how do we change what was known as a jock school [NCAA basketball champions under Jerry Tarkanian] into a great academic institution? My solution: talk about academic values, about selectivity for students, about new programs, about rigor in the way you hire and promote faculty. But that wasn't what people wanted to hear. They wanted to know if I was a good 'gal.' It became clear that my very aggressive and academic approach was not effective.

"So instead of talking about academic values, I talked about branding and marketing. I talked about Mandalay Bay, Mirage, Bally's, and UNLV, not about USC, UCLA, University of Arizona, and UNLV. That's how these folks perceive the world. Many of them don't see it in higher education terms, and I wasn't used to that mind-set."

There are more than 350 colleges and universities in New York and close to 150 in Ohio. And, as Carol explained, "Even though higher education was always a hard sell, it was never as hard a sell as it is here [where there are only two universities]. Selling the notion of research was even more difficult. Nevadans saw some monk sitting in a cell writing for two other people who look and sound just like him. They did not see [and perhaps she could not communicate] that the knowledge gained can be transferred to the greater community to solve societal problems. It was about changing values; and I wasn't always successful."

Image in Vegas is everything. As a former college newspaper editor declared, "UNLV was once known as 'a place where every stripper has the right to a decent education.'" It's an image that lingers and has proven hard to dispel. "In a town where one of the two newspapers has never been friendly to higher education and the other one is mildly positive but certainly not a strong advocate, it is very difficult to create the right public relations environment." In states like New York and Ohio, where many higher education institutions exist, "you hope to catch someone's attention. In Nevada, you spend a good deal of time trying to avoid their attention because what they want to write about is the sensational," particularly if it points to a weakness.

"In truth, this city and its culture have been a much greater challenge than I would've thought." Las Vegas is a large metropolitan area with a small-town mentality. Even today, "it's a very intense environment, very personal and very local. Despite its fast growth, the same 200 people who have run Las Vegas for the past ten to twenty years still run it." Politics are raw, rough-and-tumble, and in-your-face, and they intrude on the university.

Cross one of the powerful, and you've crossed the whole community.

The city lacks refinement—a situation Carol never quite mastered. Six years into her eleven-year presidency at UNLV, a local reporter captured her essence as a study in contradictions: "Deified and demonized. Praised and pummeled. Loved and loathed. Mostly, she's still standing." Five years later she was out, but "still standing." She has always been a woman of strong words about whom strong words are spoken. In reality, she is a woman of conviction who from the onset attracted both loyal supporters and passionate detractors.

"It's difficult when you come to a totally unrecognizable, external environment like the one I found in Nevada. Some people instantly pick up on the politics of the world they're in. It took me much longer to do that. Nevada was foreign territory. I didn't like the culture here in many ways. Even today, it can be helpful on the surface and behind your back extremely not. I've never seen quite as much full frontal hypocrisy as I've seen here. It is often anti-intellectual, and it can be downright hostile to women as leaders. Maybe I was just too dumb to see it in the other places, but it seems to me that the politics here are crude and often vindictive." In fact, the press dubbed her inauguration, which might have gone unnoticed if she had been a man, the "Coronation of Queen Carol."

"It is a cowboy culture. It is a culture of influence, who's got the most juice, who knows whom; it's not a culture of whatever's right will prevail. In my view, an awful lot of folks compromise their honesty and integrity to do the politically correct thing and to get what they need politically. They want schmoozing, glamour, and social interchange. It's a celebrity environment, and it is often superficial. My downfall as president was probably due in part to my unwillingness to compromise on those things. I will not give somebody what he or she wants or say what he or she wants to hear to get a favor because it is politically expedient to do so. I'd be dishonest with myself if I did, so I don't do it. Because I don't, I sometimes sacrifice influence.

"Politics are a daily process, especially with people who are used to doing it the Nevada way. For instance, I challenged a regent who had attacked me in the press [in 2004, nine years into her presidency] and asked, 'Why did you do that? All you had to do was call me and I would've shared the facts of the situation.' He screamed and yelled at me and said, 'You've attacked me; wait'll you see what I do to you next.' Somebody else would've just put up with it as typical Nevadan regent behavior, but [as president] I tried to correct things if they were inaccurate. Doing so was really risky because these people were my bosses."

By her own admission, aspects of her persona make her vulnerable to attack. "I am very direct and that makes some people uncomfortable, and they get defensive." As one observer noted, "You either like her or you don't like her. And people who don't like her, *really* don't like her." She's intense. She's blunt. She's driven. As a colleague put it, "She's commanding and loyal, doesn't suffer fools well or make small talk, demands loyalty, and is extremely intelligent." Tenacity is both her greatest strength and her worst weakness. "I'm not a patient person. I'm very aggressive. I don't give up."

Her steep learning curve as an external president and her intense push toward campus-wide planning initiatives caused students to see her as sometimes unengaged and her detractors to see her as hard-nosed and somewhat aloof. In her early years she had little time to venture from her office and rarely walked the campus, both activities the previous president did often, sometimes to the exclusion of effective campus management. She admits that the higher she went, the less contact she had with the reason she got into education—the students. "I believe that the most important thing we do as a university is to develop individual talent and intellectual capital. But in terms of how I behaved as president on a daily basis, cultivation of individuals was much less important. I couldn't think about one person; I had to think about 28,000 and the enterprise in its entirety."

In the end, it seems that her status as a woman, coupled with her distaste for politics and her initial misread of the Las Vegas culture, haunted her throughout her presidency. As one regent put it, "For a lot of people, Dr. Harter [as] a man would be [viewed as] an aggressive and strong leader, but as a woman, to too many people she is a bitch."

Her presidency, however, had its rewards. The community's creative spirit fit her style, and she was able to capitalize on it. "The upside of this rough-and-ready culture is that it's extremely entrepreneurial; there are no holds barred. You can move an agenda faster here than you can in most academic cultures and in most cities. In a city where decision making is quick, creativity is high, and few bureaucratic obstacles exist, that affects the culture of the institution. Certainly it does administratively. We've been able to move far more quickly at UNLV than I ever would've been able to in New York or Ohio. It just is a different kind of place."

Throughout her presidency, the position became not only her career but her life. "You never stop being a university president. There's nobody else who has that responsibility. I didn't have time for hobbies, I just worked." Carol possessed an unerring sense of direction, harbored no doubts about the rightness of what she was doing, and believed her actions made a difference. "Being self-assured allows you to make decisions. You have to be decisive. You can't be wishy-washy. And when you're committed to a cause and it's not your ego driving it, people see your passion and become committed to it; it generates enthusiasm. There are a lot of good leaders who are good managers, but because they're not passionate, they're not great leaders."

She contends, "You have to be willing to put yourself out there. You have to take risks, but they must be responsible risks— ethical risks. If you are not willing to take risks and you fail to encourage entrepreneurial thinking in faculty and administrators, you squelch creativity and innovation. You can always say you made a mistake if you make the wrong decision, learn from it, and move on." When Carol arrived at UNLV, she had little experience with high-profile athletic programs. Although she had spent almost twenty years at a Division I university, her presidency was at a Division III college, and she underestimated the importance placed on big-time athletics at UNLV—clearly an error on her part. She recovered nicely by turning a perceived deficiency into a position of national leadership within the National Collegiate Athletic Association (NCAA), serving on the NCAA Board of Directors three times and the NCAA board executive committee twice. She was the first woman university president in the nation to do so.

She strongly believes that you must always move forward. "Examining historical precedent is fine if you are writing an organization's history. History is simply an accumulation of past events; it tells you little about the future. It does not provide a good starting point for making decisions that are supposed to move an organization in a new direction. You can't live in the status quo; it's not a viable place. You certainly can't go back to the past. We acquired 630 acres for a north campus—am I going to build that campus? Hell no, but in a hundred years they're going to thank whomever was back there and thought to get that land. It has nothing to do with being self-serving, it has to do with the future of this institution, this city, and this valley."

Carol arrived at the university in 1995 when the institution was less than forty years old. In the first eight years of her presidency, 500 of the 800 faculty were new hires who came with different aspirations. They understood they would "have to work harder here, but I cannot tell you how many people's first sentence was, 'The challenges here are wonderful.'" Between 1995 and 2006, UNLV embarked on planned academic growth, developing more than 100 new degree programs (over half of them at the graduate level, with Ph.D.s in all academic and some professional disciplines) and opening schools of law, architecture, dental medicine, and nursing. The university established three new campuses, built seventeen buildings, including a student union, a recreation center, residence halls, and buildings to house urban affairs and science and engineering. Perhaps the most celebrated campus addition was the Lied Library, which opened in 2001. The story goes that Harter made sure the library was bigger than the basketball arena by one square foot. In reality, it is bigger by more than 1,000 square feet, and "it is bigger on purpose: to shift the focus away from the kind of school UNLV was and toward its new identity." In Carol's eleven years, UNLV, in effect, has been transformed "from a basketball school that dabbled in academics" to a major research university, and Lied Library stands as a prominent symbol of its purposeful shift. Such change takes money. Since 1982, the UNLV Foundation has raised almost $700 million, about 80% of which entered UNLV's coffers during Harter's presidency. In 2007 student leaders persuaded the Board of Regents to name a large classroom building for her.

So, what went wrong? Simply put, system chancellor Jim Rogers—a lawyer and a multimillionaire with no higher education experience except as a philanthropist—whose disdain for Harter was barely concealed from the time he took over in 2005, forced her out of the presidency two years before her planned retirement. He accused her of micromanaging the institution, surrounding herself with too many like-minded people, and not paying attention to diversity issues. Carol admits she did not delegate as well as she should have, but discounts charges of cronyism. In many respects her ability to get results renders the chancellor's management-related charges somewhat suspect. Concerns about minority student retention and parity in terms of the proportion of minority faculty compared to the proportion of minority students surface on almost all college campuses, including UNLV. Even so, almost 50% of the 2007 spring graduating class were classified as minority, and although the proportion of minority students (33%) is higher than the proportion of minority faculty (20%), the ratio is closer at UNLV than it is on many university campuses, again perhaps bringing Rogers's accusations into question.

As one observer noted, "Jim's problem was simple. She [Carol] wouldn't take crap from anybody, particularly him. She knows more about education than he does, and she won't back down." In effect, Rogers, who brags that he is "more than a trifle dictatorial," found his university president "too headstrong and iron-fisted." Regents, who for the most part cowered in the wake of

Rogers's relentless onslaught, now timidly suggest that he's been "running roughshod" and that "her departure was not handled in the classiest or most professional way."

Carol says she misses her old job. "In some ways, I've disappeared. When you're a president for seventeen years, it's not just what you do, it's who you are." But she also subscribes to the three Rs of leadership: resilience, reflection, and rebounding.

For Carol, resilience is a mainstay. "Resilience means you have to be thick skinned and able to move beyond things that drive you crazy—otherwise you are vulnerable to being hurt physically and emotionally. If you don't take care of yourself, no one else will. I exercise rigorously every day and have a weight-resistance trainer, take an occasional weekend break, and see a physician regularly. It's a matter of self-preservation."

Emotional support and intelligent sounding boards also fortify resilience. "I have a terrifically supportive husband. We advise each other well. He has a wonderful sense of fairness and believes in equality in child rearing." She suggests, "When you are a woman who is president and also happens to be a wife and a mother, you work at balancing your personal and professional lives all the time. Even after all these years (close to fifty), Mike and I still work at it." It's a tough balance. Each of her presidencies resulted in marital ups and downs and the need to adjust to an extended commuter relationship.

Mentors and outside advisors also influenced Carol. "I was fortunate that the president of Ohio University whom I worked under was such a good teacher. All my mentors were great people, but they were White males. When I had to figure out, 'Am I going to this Boy Scout meeting?' 'Can I get home to make cookies for this PTA event?' or 'What dress should I wear to this event?' they didn't have a clue. If I asked, they'd look at me like—'Huh? Call my wife.'"

She also participated in professional organizations that bring presidents together and found that helpful. "Sharing with others, letting your hair down, getting useful advice from people who have been there, too—these are important experiences. There is only one president on a campus; you sometimes feel isolated and lonely because there are no peers in whom you can fully confide or from whom you can ask for collegial advice. Other presidents are enormously helpful in that regard, and we all seek that camaraderie."

Throughout her presidency Carol had little time to reflect but values the opportunities she gets. As she says, "It's what rejuvenates you. It not only helps you tell your story, it helps you make sense of it." She was born in 1941 in Brooklyn, New York, but was raised, along with her sister, on Long Island by a strong, domineering, and strict Irish father and a somewhat less conservative, artistically inclined mother. When she graduated from high school, women had fewer choices professionally than they do today—"teachers and nurses, basically. I was told by a faculty member, 'Don't major in chemistry; women don't do that. Major in English.' So I did.

"In the '50s and '60s, women didn't have much freedom, particularly if you came from a traditional Irish family. At college, I enjoyed partying probably too much, but, boy, was it fun." She dropped out of college at nineteen to get married, but went back to school at Harpur College (today's Binghamton University) when her two sons were young. She ended up pursuing a master's and a doctorate in English at Harpur because she could earn money as a graduate assistant. She did apply to Cornell's Ph.D.

program, but was rejected because faculty in the program believed she would get pregnant again.

Times have changed. Today, Carol worries that women are increasingly delaying having families (children) until their midthirties and early forties, mid-career in terms of faculty members and administrators. Doing so "curtails their ability to move up because they have other priorities that command their time. When they 'stop out' or slow down at this crucial point in their careers, they lose momentum. If you want to be a college president, it has to be your entire focus. I was a president for seventeen years and that's mainly because I had my first child at the age of twenty and my second shortly after. I never took a presidency until my younger son was in law school. If I had waited until my thirties to have my children, I wouldn't be here today."

She continues to reflect, "You have to be single-minded about the presidency. If you are married, you have to have a spouse who can stand up to the pressure, be supportive of you, can take the long hours, be content to be in the background, and be willing to subvert his career to yours. The presidency is all-consuming, so you must make a conscious decision to pursue it in lieu of something else. You have to prepare yourself through experience and by taking advantage of professional development like Harvard's educational management program."

Rebounding is perhaps what Carol does best. Although she still occasionally grieves over the loss of her presidency, she has bounced back. As one reporter put it, "In an ironic turn of events, she's ended up in the building that bears the name of Jim Rogers, who chased her out of the presidency, heading a project that she loves." The project is the Black Mountain Institute (BMI).

Founded in 2006, BMI is an international center for global discourse on today's most pressing issues. BMI's programs include the Cities of Asylum project; a writers' think tank, called the Forum on Contemporary Cultures (FCC); and a Forum Fellows program. The Cities of Asylum offers refuge to persecuted writers whose voices are muffled by censorship, or who are living with the threat of imprisonment or assassination. Under the auspices of the Institute (BMI), Las Vegas was the first of five U.S. cities to join the worldwide alliance and, in 2007, hosted its third writer—an Iranian woman novelist. FCC is a lecture and symposium series that brings international writers and public intellectuals to Las Vegas to engage the university and community through readings, debates, panels, interviews, and meetings. And the Forum Fellows program offers nine-month residencies for up to three writers and scholars whose work reflects international themes and interests.

As she invests her enthusiasm in this new passion, Carol sees more time for reflecting and writing and for supporting her husband Mike's career as CEO of Touro University-Nevada. For a hard-driving, fully committed individual like Carol Harter, shaping the fledgling Black Mountain Institute into an international literary powerhouse seems an apt challenge. Her statement, "Creating things gives me great personal satisfaction," truly captures the essence of this unique pioneer—who is still standing.

BIBLIOGRAPHICAL NOTES

Carol C. Harter's story derives from multiple sources. Included in the list are interview transcripts; vitae; *State of the University* addresses by Harter; internal University of Nevada, Las Vegas, news releases; University of Nevada, Las Vegas, websites, including the Black Mountain Institute website; and presidential columns in the *UNLV Magazine*. Other sources are Suzan Dibella, "On a More Personal Note," *UNLV Magazine* (Spring 2001, 16–23); Lynn Goya, "Nevada's Legacy Builders," *Luxury Las Vegas* (April 2007, 73–77); Anne Roark, "'An 'Entrepreneurial' Way of Thinking," *National CrossTalk* 11(2) (Spring 2003); Christine Littlefield, "Passing the Test," *Las Vegas Sun* (June 24, 2005) and "The Ouster of Carol Harter," *Las Vegas Sun* (February 2, 2006); "Six Questions about Harter," *Las Vegas Weekly* (February 2, 2003); Ky Plaskon, "UNLV President Steps Down," *Las Vegas NOW.com* (January 30, 2006); Steve Bornfeld, "An Interview with Carol Harter," *Las Vegas Life* (March 2001); and Carol C. Harter, "Tough Mind, Warm Heart," edited by Karen Doyle Walton, in *Against the Tide* (pp. 121–134), Bloomington, IN: Phi Delta Kappa Foundation (1996).

SIX

MAKING DIVERSITY WORK

Mamie Howard-Golladay
Sullivan County Community College

"I WAS BORN IN MISSISSIPPI, but my family moved to southern Alabama when I was little. I grew up in the Jim Crow era of the 1950s and 1960s. Neither of my parents graduated from high school. I was the first one in my family to graduate from college. There were six of us children, stair steps, with a year separating our ages. I'm the oldest. When I was five, I started taking care of my baby brother. I pretty much raised the other kids while our mother worked. When I was twelve, I started working nights in a restaurant. I worked at one restaurant or another until I graduated high school.

"We were poor, but we didn't know it. And, despite being poor, our mom instilled in us the belief that we could do anything we set our minds to. She constantly told us to rely on our own abilities to make it in this world and never to consider ourselves victims of anything. She stressed the importance of taking advantage of every opportunity that came our way.

"Because mother and dad both worked, we didn't get a lot of individual attention at home. I was always a bright little kid, so in school, I wanted to be number one because it brought me accolades and approval from my teachers. I had huge dreams of going to college, but because of segregation, my career choices were very limited. I went to the teacher education program at a predominantly Black college for one semester but decided that it was not for me. I got married and had a son, and although I was happy, something was missing.

"When my baby was six months old, I said, 'I can't just sit around. I've got to do something.' I put on my little blue suit and went to an employment agency. The agent sent me to an office where they needed a secretary. This White man took one look at me and said, 'The position is filled.' I went straight back to the employment agent and said, 'Why did you send me there when they've already filled the position?' He picked up the phone and called that office. The man I had just met with told him the position was still vacant. The employment agent said, 'I just sent you someone.' The man on the other end hung up the phone. So the employment agent sent me to the hospital to take the nurse assistant test, which I aced."

Mamie quickly moved up the ranks in that hospital, receiving her L.P.N., R.N., and B.S.N. while working full time. She was supported and mentored along the way by a White male hospital administrator who saw and believed in her talents. "When I completed my bachelor's degree, he had a candid conversation with me about my next steps. Since I was the only nurse at that hospital with a bachelor's degree, the director of nursing position should have been mine. He told me the medical staff was not ready for a Black director of nurses. The hurt was deep and searing. I realized that no matter how much education I had received, I still did not measure up in this society because of my race. It gave me an intimate understanding of discrimination and the issues that surround diversity.

"We filter everything we do through culture, whether it's bad or good. My cultural upbringing has most certainly had an effect on the way I lead. I find that I'm very aware of and sensitive to situations in which individuals might experience disadvantages or limitations because of who they are or what they represent. I believe that it helps me be a more effective leader because, once you understand the culture, you can decide if and how it needs reshaping.

"Sullivan County Community College is one of the most diverse community colleges in the State University of New York (SUNY) system. Thirty-four percent of our students are Latino, African American, or Asian American—rural, urban, and suburban. In contrast, when I arrived, 98% of its approximately 100 full- and part-time faculty were White. At that time the SUNY student opinion surveys indicated that because most of the administration, faculty, and staff were majority race, minority students believed the college was not sensitive to their needs. I am the first female and the first African American president at Sullivan. The previous administrations didn't seem to look at issues of culture and diversity in the same way I do. If you're not living it and you're not in touch with it, it's tough to understand what changes need to be made and how best to make them."

The college, which is in the Catskill Mountains sixteen miles from the legendary Woodstock Festival site, opened its doors to county residents in 1963. Today, about 40% of its 1,630 students come from outside Sullivan County. "To be sure, we've definitely dealt with culture issues, and quite often they have been student-centered. Many of our students are from New York City. They bring their loud music, loud voices, and urban culture with them into this quiet rural environment. It sometimes causes friction with the local students. Some of the students from the city have never been in a rural setting. The local students teased them, telling them that the deer would run them down and attack them. It was obviously a joke, but it upset some of the 'city' students. Now in orientation we talk about the wildlife in Sullivan and valuing the beauty and quiet of the area. Even so, when the Levine Residence Hall opened in 2003, there were problems because we were not used to having students on campus 24/7. We had 320 freshmen all away from home for the first time. They were pulling the fire alarms, partying, making all kinds of loud noise, and leaving trash everywhere. It was a nightmare. We didn't have the staff and procedures in place to handle it. But we got help from the other SUNY schools that have residence halls, and we learned fast.

"It's been interesting to try to make sure that the culture of the campus is welcoming to both city and local students. My administration has attempted to shape a culture that provides a rich experience for all of them. One of my first commitments was to invest in the student services area and add additional student activities personnel. Over the years we have hired a diverse student activities staff who help students plan events that honor and celebrate their backgrounds. We have a very active cultural series with plays, lectures, bands, and musicals. We have Caribbean night, Latin dance groups, slam poetry meets. We have AWARE, a club for Adults Who Are Returning to Education, and we sponsor Elderhostel in the summer. We also have a large Jewish population in the area whose influence is represented as well. Even food service offers meals once a week that reflect a specific culture. Our courses also address culture. For example, we require a freshman orientation seminar, which includes a module that focuses on cultural differences and learning how to treat and live with others. In addition, we have an SCCC Campus Code of Civility written by students and faculty.

"I want our students to see ethnic and gender diversity at work in all areas here at Sullivan. I am willing to confront discrimination head on. I don't go looking for it, but when I see it I deal with it. I don't believe in covering it up or putting it aside. This approach makes some majority individuals uncomfortable because they don't want to acknowledge that racism or sexism exists. I'm not saying they condone certain behavior; they just find it uncomfortable to address it and want to avoid confrontation. I believe that approach stifles opportunities to learn about others.

"I prefer to talk about it openly so we can learn from each other's perspectives, to ask, 'What do you see that I don't see? Because what I see is clearly discrimination.' In my third annual evaluation, one of my evaluators called me an ice queen, and someone else said I was overbearing. I asked my board how being an ice queen was relevant to my job and whether my male predecessors were called overbearing or ice kings? I explained that I felt these descriptions were sexist and probably racist.

"Stereotypes can, however, work in your favor. Because people sometimes expect Black women to be aggressive, we can get away with being the kind of leaders we need to be. If I say something in a meeting and people don't listen or they dismiss what I say, I have to assert myself. They might think, 'Well, there's that Black woman with her big mouth,' but they listen because they expect me to be a big mouth—that is the stereotype at work. I have to do the job. I have to lead. I'm going to try to get as much input as I can, but when the day is over, it's all on my head. I'm not going to worry about whether you think I'm too aggressive or too overbearing.

"I'm a fairly tall woman and I have a bit of presence. I think that plays into it. I can stand up or walk into a room and I'm noticed. I like being a woman, being feminine, but I am also an educational leader and I play different roles at different times.

Sometimes I must be hard-nosed and play the heavy. Other times I can go easier. Over the years I have done a lot of 'tall talking' for people here to understand why we had to make certain changes. I was able to get them to listen because of who I am. I'm not so sure someone else would have been able to, but they respect my life experience and figure maybe I know what I'm talking about.

"I've been accused of hiring only women, but I don't. I hire the most qualified person. For example, I had young male students say to me, 'I don't want to go to the counseling center because there are only women there.' When we had the opportunity to hire in counseling, I shared their perspective with the screening committee. To some of them, counselors are supposed to be women, so they looked for the best-qualified women candidates. When they sent me an all-female slate, I sent it back. Their revised list included qualified males, and we were able to hire a young man in the counseling center. It was my responsibility as institutional leader to help them be aware of the need and their possible bias.

"Personally, I know that I am only as good as the team I work with. I must have a capable and loyal team. It took me a while, but I've put together an excellent leadership team. When I came here, there were men in all but one of the leadership positions. Over time, I replaced two male vice presidents and promoted several well-deserving women. Because I am a woman, the rumor went around that I only wanted to work with women. Of course, that's not true. I do have two female vice presidents, but my two deans are men. I also have two men and two women division chairs.

"The vice president of administrative affairs was the only woman on the previous president's leadership team, which I think must have been tough. She is brilliant, but we had to work on changing her style a bit to fit the new team. It is not that I want everybody around me thinking, speaking, and sounding like me and giving me the same advice. I want to work with people who will share information with me, no matter what the message is, good or bad. I want to hear everything that's going on. I really abhor working with someone who only tells me the good things. I want people who think differently. We can disagree and that's fine. But we can also create new ideas and that's great. The only way you can be effective is if you have a team of people who are different, individual, and speak their minds.

"I also want people to be comfortable enough to let the president know when they've messed up. I know that I must set the example by being willing to open up, examine myself critically. It is safe and easy to say, 'Okay, I'm good at this and I do this well.' When you are in the presidency, it can be very hard to say, 'I have this weakness.' But to be effective you should allow the people who work with you to know that you have vulnerabilities, that you know you're not omnipotent but human, and that you make mistakes. You have to allow yourself to say, 'Maybe I don't know the right way to go,' and be willing to ask others.

"Communication is such a complicated process. It entails not only sending a message but ensuring that the message is received the way you wanted it to be heard. Listening is the key. You have to listen to know what actually got transmitted and how it was received. One way of listening and communicating is placing people in roles where you can talk with them on a regular basis. When I came to Sullivan, there were no faculty or staff on the administrative council. I changed the name to President's Cabinet and added staff and faculty from all of the key areas. Now a wider group of people hear firsthand what's going on, feel a part of what's going on, and take that information back to their constituent groups. It's worked out very well. It also cuts down on speculation and rumormongering."

On November 8, 2007, a seventeen-year-old freshman died on campus. It was also the anniversary of the drowning death of Mamie's son and only child. "The rumor mill started quickly. Personally, I had to hold it together for the whole college, all the while thinking, 'Why on this day?' I couldn't believe this was happening. This student was not much older than Tim was when he died. You have to show some emotion when it's appropriate. Your staff needs to know you are human, that you have feelings just like they do, but overdoing can be trouble, for women or men. Either extreme—crying or screaming and shouting at people, even when they have really messed up—can be a problem. In this instance I had to work through my own emotions and, at the same time, keep everybody going and get information out.

"The grapevine had it that something violent had happened to the student, although all we knew was that he was playing video games with another student in the dormitory and collapsed. Some students were angry because they thought the ambulance was slow in arriving. Others thought the peace officer who gave the young man CPR didn't know how to do it because the 911 operator was giving him instructions. I explained that this is the protocol for that kind of emergency call. We talked to keep the students calm, answered questions from the community at large, and quelled the rumors. Later, the autopsy found that the student had gone into cardiac arrest because of an enlarged heart, a condition of which he was unaware."

Dispelling half-truths and ill-conceived ideas in a crisis is paramount. But informal information networks can also serve a proactive purpose. "People throughout the organization make sure I know what's going on. It is so ironic to have someone, usually a clerical person, come in and say, 'I know I'm gossiping, but I really have to tell you this.' Often I say, 'Yes, you are gossiping. I appreciate your telling me this but don't keep spreading it around, okay?' Sometimes, I've put information on the grapevine. For example, we reorganized last year, going from four divisions to five, creating a vocational division. Earlier, I floated the idea through the grapevine to see what the reaction would be. In this instance, the message got really warped, suggesting that we were getting rid of one division and replacing it with a new one. When it came back to me, it helped me know where the problems might lie. I could tell that certain people were anxious about the possibility of this type of change, and some even saw it as a personal attack. We let the issue die down, and before we officially discussed reorganization, we were able to work through many of the issues that seemed to cause concern. The reorganization ended up being the easiest I've ever witnessed in my whole career. It was amazing. We presented the initial plan in October and, by the following September, the reorganization was completed—programs, budget, and people—all in place. I attribute a lot of its success to preparation and readiness.

"When I came to Sullivan, the college seemed to be up on the hill alone. We didn't seem to have a strong, close connection to the community. Everywhere I traveled people talked about how they *used to* come to the campus for different events. Sullivan has a renowned culinary arts program, one of only seven postsecondary institutions in New York State with programs accredited by the American Culinary Federation. People in the community came to campus to have meals prepared by the students in those programs. It was a nice way of getting the community on campus, but we were no longer using it to our advantage. I made it a priority to get the community coming back on the campus. We held three community forums to get some of them involved. I invited the local town councils and school superintendents to campus for dinners. We've gotten the legislators back on campus with informal legislative breakfasts and other events."

These types of events not only engage the community with the college, they also provide good development opportunities. "We have a foundation that is very active, but it wasn't thinking big. When we decided to build the residence hall, I put together a prospectus and went to see a local billionaire whom I had read about but never met. We sat and talked and I asked him for $12 million. I will always remember what he said, 'No one from the college has ever asked me for any money.' When I told the college leadership team what he had said, they responded, 'Oh, yes, we did. We asked for and he gave us $200,000.' I laughed. In his mind that was not money; it was pocket change. He ended up giving us $3 million for the residence hall project and helped us launch our *Start of Something Great Capital Campaign.* He's been a good friend to the college ever since and has supported us in other initiatives.

"This campus is forty-five years old. It hadn't added any new facilities until I came on board. We needed to look at things differently." Soon after Mamie became president in 1998, SCCC became the first community college on the East Coast to open a cybercafé. SCCC continued its commitment to technological innovations by establishing a wireless campus network and offering online and interactive television courses in a partnership with SUNY at New Paltz that makes four-year bachelor degree programs available on the SCCC campus. In addition, SCCC was the only U.S. college to offer on-site courses to the soldiers in Tikrit, Iraq. Army personnel with advanced degrees taught the courses for free to approximately 100 students at Forward Operating Base Speicher.

In spring 2007, another SCCC innovation was highlighted at the National Sustainable Design Expo in Washington, D.C. The project, known as G-Tech, is a planned sixty-acre, green technology park and a partnership among the college, county, and private businesses. The first of its kind in New York, it will be a place to prepare students for "green collar" technology jobs. Howard-Golladay stated, "This little college is really in the forefront of the sustainability movement, not only in the Hudson Valley, but also in the state of New York. Businesses locating in the park must produce, research, and manufacture green products. The project is a great fit for the campus because SCCC already has noncredit programs in sustainable energy, will soon operate two wind turbines, and uses a geothermal system that provides heating and air conditioning for the campus."

Changing the culture through innovative programming and practices has helped SCCC grow and expand in ways that make it not only more environmentally sustainable but more economically viable as well. "When I took the presidency here, the institution was in a dire situation. During the interview process they told me there was a budget shortfall, but not how serious it was. Nothing I read indicated how major that shortfall was. I started in March 1998, and in May I had to lay off fourteen people to balance the budget before the college community even got to know me. I had a real credibility setback from the beginning. Because we had a number of retirements that year after we balanced the budget, I was able to call back all of the people we laid off. That was truly fortunate, but I think it took me longer than usual to gain the trust and respect of the college because of that situation. Sometimes, you just don't know the depths of the institution's problems until you are in the job. I chose not to back away. I liked the place, the people. They were so warm and open during the interview. It just felt like a nice place to be. But the way things started out did hamper my ability to gain credibility.

"If you can't earn trust and credibility, you can't get anything done. You might as well just hang it up. Close up shop. Without it, somebody's always second-guessing you. You have to maintain the trust. In the long run it is better to say, 'I can't promise you that,' than to promise and never follow through. People remember. I always try to be honest and aboveboard, tell it like it is. They may not like it, but it is important to maintain the integrity of my word."

The issue of trust came to the fore again in February 2007 when SCCC's Professional Staff Association passed a resolution of no confidence against Howard-Golladay's administration and the SCCC Board of Trustees. The Association's members cited financial issues as a result of a decade-long decline in enrollment and "a lack of oversight" that led to low faculty and staff morale as reasons for the resolution. The Board of Trustees voiced its unanimous support for Mamie, and, a couple of months later, the Professional Staff Association agreed to "bury the hatchet" and joined Howard-Golladay in a plan to improve relations between administration and staff.

"The college had experienced a rather tight budget year. A couple of positions were abolished and employees lost their jobs. But the Association's actions took us by surprise, and before we could meet with its members to see what their issues were, they issued a statement to the media. We had to respond publicly. I had the full support of my Board of Trustees, the SUNY chancellor, and a number of my faculty and community leaders. I met privately for three hours one Sunday afternoon with four Association members. The crux of their complaint was that, with all the changes that were happening and planned for the campus [the technology park and its requisite buildings, the reorganization], as they put it, 'People believe that you care more about bricks and mortar than you do about people.' I told them, 'I want the bricks and mortar here so I don't have to face laying off people ever again.' They got it. And I understood that they felt a need for more direct communication with me. So we set up a committee of campus representatives that regularly meets directly with me to present their concerns. They don't always get what they ask for, but they do get direct access. It is not that their concerns weren't being heard before, but now the process is more formal.

"A number of other New York presidents faced no confidence votes on their own campuses at the same time as I did. Several of them left. I could have. I received invitations to apply for several lucrative positions in other states, but I decided I wanted to stay at Sullivan. The reorganization kept moving forward smoothly through all of this. In fact, things were handled so well that later I was asked to speak to the New York Community College trustees group about our experiences to provide suggestions for colleges facing similar issues.

"I came to Sullivan with skills that they were looking for in a president. In my thirty-plus years in higher education, I had been a dean of health sciences and vocational education at a community college in Michigan; dean of business, science, math, and technology at another very large community college in Maryland; a community college division chair in Florida; and a professor. I never looked at my career thinking I could be president. However, I had worked for administrators who made me realize I could do the job better than they were doing it. That is what got me to thinking I could be a CEO. Sometimes the lessons you learn about what *not* to do are the most powerful ones.

"I feel a strong commitment to the people of Sullivan County Community College. I am very aware that people see me as Ms. SCCC. I am the face of the college. Whatever happens at Sullivan, whatever I do, reflects on the organization, even my personal life." Like a growing number of working women, Mamie is in a commuter marriage. She and her second husband, Dennis Golladay, former president of Cayuga Community College (Auburn, New York) have lived in the same house for only two years of their fourteen-year marriage. "There is so much involved in the presidency. The 'space' of a commuter marriage has worked well for us. You each get to carve out time when you can do whatever it is that helps you to be reflective. I do my greatest reflection when I'm gardening; Dennis likes to build things, including furniture. When a couple sees each other every day, little things can get in the way. When we are together, we don't sweat the small stuff. If your marriage is strong and you trust the person, you can do it." Professionally Dennis's recent appointment as SUNY vice chancellor for community colleges has required Mamie as SCCC president to change the way she works with the state system to avoid any conflict of interest claims. "I used to be able to call the vice chancellor directly to ask for assistance with certain issues. But with Dennis in that job, I can't ask him to advocate for SCCC. So it's a bit tougher to get the college's issues heard.

"I am probably Sullivan's strongest advocate, not because it is my job, but because I like advocating for Sullivan. I am hard-nosed with anyone who does something detrimental to the college, but I am very proud and supportive of those who do positive things for the college. I know most of the staff is passionate about the organization, too. When I arrived here, many of the faculty had been at SCCC for twenty-five, thirty years and were starting to retire. But because they believe in the organization, they remained a part of Sullivan. They teach for us part time, and a number of them are volunteer mentors to the students living in our residence hall.

"I once read that women tend to be hired into presidencies that have a lot of challenges, while their male counterparts get more opportunities for colleges that are in good shape. And I think that's probably true. A leader sets the tone for the organization. If she appears to be rudderless, anchorless, not knowing where to go next, there will be chaos. So whether or not you have the confidence, the appearance of confidence has to be there. I

have the self-confidence. I don't think I would have gotten this
job if I didn't."

BIBLIOGRAPHICAL NOTES

Information for this profile of Mamie Howard-Golladay was created from several personal interviews with her, her vitae and her
essay, "I've Come This Far by Faith"; SCCC press releases, annual reports, college catalogue, website, and other materials; and
articles published in the *Sullivan County Democrat* (May 10,
2005), *South Florida Sun-Sentinel* (August 3, 2005), *Inside Higher
Education* (February 2, 2007), *Mid-Hudson News* (February 8,
February 20, and April 2, 2007), and the *Community College
Times* (May 11, 2007).

SEVEN

A PERFECT FIT

Martha T. Nesbitt
Gainesville State College

"WHEN A LEADER IS PASSIONATE, it's contagious. It sends the right message to the people who really make the organization work. People truly appreciate the fact that I am so passionate about this institution and what we mean to this community and to northeast Georgia. I look forward to each day at work because I'm proud to be affiliated with Gainesville. Pride builds pride. I brag a lot about the college; I tell people, as Yogi Berra once said, 'It ain't bragging if it's true.'"

And Martha Nesbitt does have bragging rights. When Gainesville had its Southern Association of Colleges and Schools (SACS) accreditation visit in 2002, the team awarded it five commendations in recognition of extraordinary performance. "I've been on SACS visits for over twenty years, and I have never heard of that happening; perhaps two, but many times there are no commendations. Our commendations for being student-focused and creating a learning-centered environment meant the most to me. These are wonderful words that actually have meaning here. The evaluation team could sense it. You cannot buy that kind of compliment."

Similarly, in 2006 Gainesville was one of four community colleges in the country to receive an award for best practices in retention from the MetLife Foundation. "What distinguishes the college is the caring and personal attitude of the faculty, which complements strong academic programs. One without the other doesn't work."

At the age of fifty-eight, Martha Nesbitt became the third president of Gainesville State College (GSC) in 1997. When the chancellor appointed her to the post, he commented, "Martha Nesbitt's entire career has been building to this presidency." After earning her baccalaureate and master's degrees from Duke University, she earned a Ph.D. in history at Georgia State University and shortly thereafter began her career at DeKalb Community College in Atlanta, Georgia, as an adjunct instructor, later becoming a full-time instructor and then chair of the social sciences division. From 1983 to 1997 she served as DeKalb's vice president for academic affairs, working concurrently as vice president of student affairs for one year and another as interim president. Her final year at DeKalb was spent on leave as special assistant to the chancellor of the University System of Georgia.

"When I was at DeKalb, the job and institution were part of me, and I was proud of all we did. I led the institution through some difficult times. When we became part of the overall Georgia public higher education system under one board of regents, not only did the faculty have to take a freeze in salary, they also lost their tenure. I worked with the faculty and administrators to set up a whole new tenure and ranking process. It was a traumatic transition, but one that was necessary for the long-term survival of the institution."

Martha learned a great deal about timing and politics at DeKalb. In 1986, she decided to try her hand at the presidency. She applied to a college in Florida, but she didn't know enough and she didn't ask for counsel. The application required six letters of reference. She asked the president to serve as one of the references. "I didn't even make the first cut. The point is I had advertised that I was interested. Somebody in the administration at DeKalb used that information to try to convince the president that I wanted his job, which I didn't. I was very supportive of the president. But the situation was used by others to bring my loyalty into question and caused me some real grief.

"Soon after this a couple of sexist male administrators collaborated to try to marginalize my role as chief academic officer. I am sure they tried to have me demoted or removed. I never confronted them directly, but I learned a lesson. I had tipped my hand too soon. If I hadn't, they wouldn't have had the ammunition."

In the next three years, she was a finalist for presidencies three times. When she applied for a presidency in Georgia in 1991, she didn't realize that Chancellor H. Dean Propst was promoting another candidate. She was devastated. "I decided that's it. I'll be a vice president for academic affairs until I retire." The opportunity several years later to work for and observe Chancellor Stephen Portch changed her mind. She applied for and won the presidency at Gainesville. "Coming to Gainesville was like getting a new lease on life. It gave me back the energy, the interest, and the passion that had begun to lessen over the years."

Gainesville State College was founded in 1964 as the only publicly supported, two-year college in northeastern Georgia. Its main campus is located in Gainesville, a city of 30,000 nestled in the Blue Ridge Mountain foothills on the shores of Lake Lanier, about one hour north of Atlanta. Although considered by some to be part of the Atlanta market, the college serves a predominantly rural, increasingly Hispanic population, providing a broad liberal arts education. A second campus is located just outside of Athens.

The state of Georgia has a tiered higher education system comprised of thirty-five two-year colleges, state colleges, and state, regional, and research universities. In 2005, Gainesville transitioned from a two-year collegiate institution to a state college. Its primary focus remains preparing students for transfer to four-year colleges, but it also offers select baccalaureate degrees in education, science, and business technology. Ninety percent of its 7,000 plus students enroll in transferable programs. The college boasts a strong retention rate, approximately 70%, and sends almost twice as many transfers to upper division programs than does any other Georgia state college. A local reporter suggests that transfer students from GSC fare better as a group than do transfers from other institutions because of the quality of instruction they receive at GSC.

In its infancy the college attracted primarily first-generation students, and, out of necessity, a student-focused institutional culture that valued individual relationships emerged. "I was so fortunate because there was such a wonderful culture and a true sense of camaraderie here when I came." Although Martha didn't have to create the culture, she does continually nurture it. "When I arrived at Gainesville, I met with every person on campus, faculty and staff. It helped me learn about the culture. As new people come in, I meet with them. I talk about our student focus and how, even though we have a great Academic Computing, Tutoring, and Testing Center, I don't want faculty saying to students, 'Oh, you go to the ACTT Center.' I want them meeting with students outside of the classroom. I set up a formal faculty mentoring system, which is very important to keeping the culture, and I make sure staff, especially the custodians and groundskeepers, feel appreciated. Everything that happens at Gainesville College, whether I like it or not, reflects on me. I don't have to worry about getting credit because I'm going to get either it or blame for what goes on here. It's important, when I can, to give credit to other people for their accomplishments. It encourages them to be more involved. I really care about the people who make this institution work, and I think for the most part that comes through. We don't have a great deal of turnover here. People come and they stay.

"I also inherited a strong administrative team." And to ensure that it stayed healthy, she immediately provided its members with a "comfort zone" in which to disagree with her, and with each other, as professionals. "If people do not speak out and are not candid and open, the institution loses. There's really not much point in having a discussion if somebody's intimidated from the outset."

Her leadership philosophy promotes collaboration, team building, the generation of new solutions to old problems, and a willingness to explore untapped opportunities. "I value the individual more than individuality. When I think of individuality, I think of John Wayne. I like John Wayne, but we want people to work together. I don't micromanage. I don't tell people what to do. I use persuasion. I throw out my ideas to a group and then listen. I rarely make a decision without feedback. I firmly believe that if I do other people's work, I undermine them, and I certainly don't help them grow. I don't help them become a vital part of the organization. I understand that we can't all be equally creative, but we can encourage people to come up with new ideas and then be open to them. In fact, it was my vice president of academic affairs and an associate vice president who said, 'Martha, we need to go over to Athens [to establish the second campus in 2003].' We did, and it's been very good for the institution.

"It's not my job to make all the decisions; it's my job to be competent. We know the importance of good communication, human relations skills, enthusiasm, and commitment, but if you're not competent, it doesn't work. Being nice does not make up for incompetence. If you're not competent, it's very hard to gain the respect of the people with whom you work. It doesn't take long for them to figure out whether you know what you're doing. If you're not competent, you're not credible."

She contends that, for presidents, being competent means understanding what higher education is all about, where your sector fits in, how your system works, and what the issues are—whether it's the importance of remedial education, the role of honors programs in two-year colleges, or being informed about facilities management. "I'm certainly not a facilities manager, but I know a whole lot more about facilities than I did in 1997. I don't write the budget, but I am familiar with the budget in general, and I work well with my chief financial officer. That's a person, by the way, who can get you in trouble faster than anybody else."

Awards and recognition over the years attest to Martha's competency. In 1995, she was selected Outstanding Woman of the Year by the American Association of Women in Community Colleges, and in 2004 she was chosen Business Woman of the Year by the American Business Woman's Association. Perhaps her proudest moment, however, occurred in 2007 when GSC established an endowed scholarship fund in her honor.

Although Martha truly believes in the strength of team leadership, she admits that presidents do have power. "One of the funniest things I had to deal with when I first came was that I wasn't happy with the grounds. I suggested we plant azaleas in the quadrangle. The next week they're out there planting azaleas. Somebody came to me and said, 'Who in the world told them to plant azaleas? They'll never survive out there.' And I said, 'I did.' I grew up in South Georgia and azaleas live in full sun quite well there. But, these were a different kind of azalea. I learned an important lesson—I had to be careful about what I said. If I wanted azaleas, I could have azaleas, if for no other reason than that I was president. So, it's about using your power appropriately. And sparingly.

"Your credibility comes, at least in part, from how you use your power. You have to share it." In her estimation sharing power requires communication. "It's a constant challenge for me to communicate as broadly as I can and then encourage the people I work with to do the same. We need to be transparent about why we make decisions.

"One decision I made was very problematic. We moved our business division from the building it was in to another building because we needed some additional space. It was the smallest division, and if I moved anybody else, I'd be moving half or a third of a division. We discussed it quite a bit in the Executive Council, and I told its members not to say anything about it until we had actually made up our mind and talked to the unit about it. But somebody on the Council leaked it, and the librarian said to one of the businesspeople, 'I hear you're moving to the CE Building.' That's how the division found out about it. Its people were not happy, and at that point we had to do damage control.

"If I had gone to them to begin with and said, 'We're *thinking* about moving you,' they would have said, 'We don't want to move.' If I had said, 'You're moving,' they would have replied, 'Why did you come to us if you've already made up your mind?'

If the leak hadn't occurred, I would've gone to them and said, 'We have considered these alternatives; if you can think of a better one, let me know.' Even members of the business unit, after the fact, couldn't come up with an alternative that wasn't harmful to the culture of the institution. Moving the unit was one of those actions that took an executive decision. But the process broke down. It was a disaster. I still wrestle with the best way to have handled it. I do not regret the decision; I regret the way it was handled."

Even though Martha works hard at keeping everyone informed, she sometimes still gets accused of having a hidden agenda. A case in point: "The Executive Council makes many campus decisions, and we think that because we decide something, Council members go back and tell their people, and their people tell their people; but it doesn't always happen that way. The word wasn't getting out. People began to think we had secrets. So I've started doing meeting notes that I send out to the college community."

Communication is just the tip of the proverbial iceberg. It takes a great deal of stamina to face the challenges that tax education leaders today. She notes, "It's not about being an extrovert, it's about having a lot of energy." Like many of her contemporaries, when Martha is at work, she is very focused on what she's doing. As president her work doesn't end when she leaves the college. She takes work home. She's out in the community. But, she says, "I never feel like I'm on stage. When I'm in the grocery store, I don't feel that I have to act like I'm president of Gainesville College. I'm Martha Nesbitt. I think part of that is just being comfortable." She enjoys her job, and that enjoyment energizes her. Although she says, "I can't really talk about my work as part of my life because my work is my life," she does have other interests, including two married children and three grandchildren.

"I seek a balance as much as possible. I take off one week each year and travel with my husband of forty-four years, who is retired. And I may take off a day here and there and play golf. I make sure that I get the rest I need, eat properly, and exercise. Leaders who don't jeopardize their physical and emotional health, and they're not good for the institution. We all know people who burned out. They didn't have what I call balance in the long run.

"You experience rough knocks in this job, like when we lost the new student center due to budget cuts. Had I not been in public the day I heard the news, I might've cried." It takes emotional stamina to overcome such disappointments. But she contends that personnel issues are the biggest challenges for any leader—"knowing when to be compassionate and when to be firm. It's nice to hope that people are going to shape up when they've been told what needs to be done, but some people aren't able and others aren't willing, and you have to deal with them the best you can. It's the most emotional part of being a leader."

Emotions do matter. Nesbitt firmly believes that as president it's important for her to indicate when she's really happy and when she's disappointed. It puts a human face on a leader. She suggests that a leader occasionally needs to show what she calls controlled anger. "It's a judgment call. But, there have been times when something was sufficiently provoking for me to say that it really made me angry. Not lose control. Never lose control." She adds, "A sense of humor also helps. It relieves the stress."

She believes the presidency must reflect an individual's entire persona. She maintains that presidents must look and sound confident. If not, "you won't inspire much confidence in the people you work with. But confidence is a gray area. You can be overconfident and not ask for help when you need it." To counter any such tendency, she argues that leaders must make an inward journey, discovering not only their strengths, but their insecurities and unnatural fears as well. "Our integrity depends on it.

"Integrity has to do with knowing yourself, knowing your personality, and being true to yourself. We all have to learn how to say things diplomatically and professionally, but those around me need to know that this is Martha Nesbitt. This is not some facade. I mean what I say. I give you reasons why I do what I do. If I didn't have integrity, people wouldn't think I'm honest and trust what I'm doing. It's about being authentic.

"Trust is so important. You cannot command trust. You build it. No one trusts you just because you are president. I need that trust because there are going to be times when I make mistakes. Every leader makes mistakes. Nobody's infallible. Sometimes the smartest thing I can do is apologize. The fact that people trust that I'm trying to do the right thing, that I'm not out for personal gain, lends power to my position as president. Self-promotion can be a real stumbling block for leaders when those around them say, 'Well, she's doing that because it's going to help her, but it's not going to help the institution.' People have to trust my motivation. I feel I'm doing a good job. If the time comes when I don't have that self-assurance, it will be time to step down."

As Gainesville's first female president and one of only eight in the Georgia system, Martha worries that there are not enough women in the pipeline. "I fear that some of our best minds are going into business and industry because they can make so much more money. For me, the lifestyle that working in higher education affords is worth the trade-off. But we really have to encourage young women in education to aspire to administrative positions. My concern is that many women aren't willing to make the sacrifices that they perceive are involved with being president or vice president. They see long hours, challenges, stress."

She points out that women are sometimes conflicted about seeking leadership positions, on the one hand, and wanting to be married and raise families, on the other. Deciding where their balance lies and what is most important may mean they wait until their children are older, when the demands at home are less, before they go into administrative positions. Martha's children were in high school when she became a vice president. "I know a lot of men help at home and with children, but unless you're lucky enough to have a househusband, the primary responsibility for these tasks still falls to women.

"I also think women still need to be assured that they can be gentle leaders who know how to ask for advice. A perception exists out there that when you ask for advice, you're showing weakness. And that's really not what it's all about. Leadership is about relationships, working with people, getting people to work with you; you simply can't do it all. Women have a tremendous amount of potential as leaders to really influence an institution because they have been socialized to be concerned about relationships, about creating win-win solutions. I want them to stay the course and not feel like they have to be perceived as strong top-down managers."

She suggests that today women can start on the path to higher education leadership from any position within the college—

faculty or mid-level administration—but they do need experience. They must take advantage of any professional development opportunities they have, such as attending leadership workshops and conferences, getting involved in their professional organizations, and engaging in professional activities that look good on a resumé. "These are good building tools."

Martha engaged in such activities, but she was also fortunate to have been raised in a family where education and business activities were important. Her father was a civil engineer who owned a building business. Her mother, a community college graduate, helped with the business and later became involved in government programs, ending her career as an international trade fair manager for the U.S. Department of Agriculture. Both parents served as significant role models for Martha and her brother, who is president of a major distributing company in South Carolina. In Martha's case, her mother's guidance was particularly important. "She was a major influence in my life. She always supported and encouraged me in whatever I did."

In 1997 Martha Nesbitt went to Gainesville College and, for over ten years, it has remained a perfect fit. A recent article in the *Gainesville Times* boldly states: "[Nesbitt] loves students and she is dedicated to ensuring that GSC does everything it can to ensure they graduate or transfer to another school. . . . She is tirelessly involved in the community [because] she believes that our community is better when everyone participates. [She] points to her staff, the college's faculty, an involved community, and even the students, themselves, as the reasons for GSC successes. And she's right to a point—all these groups play a role. But Nesbitt deserves a hearty pat on the back too. Her vision and leadership have propelled GSC for a decade and the future is bright."

Martha expresses her feelings about her relationship with the institution this way: "I thank God every day that He didn't give me those other presidencies, because I wouldn't be in Gainesville. It's a great community and college. This will be my last position. It's a great way to end my career."

BIBLIOGRAPHICAL NOTES

Martha T. Nesbitt's story resulted from in-depth interviews, her vitae, and perusal of the Gainesville State College website and other college publications and documents.

EIGHT

COMMUNICATING COMMITMENT

Pamela Sue Shockley-Zalabak
University of Colorado, Colorado Springs

IN OCTOBER 2006, allegations arose that the University of Colorado at Colorado Springs (UCCS) was penalizing its students when military duties called them away from the classroom. Chancellor Pamela Sue Shockley-Zalabak acted purposefully. As the university newspaper reported, "Just to be sure a problem didn't exist, the chancellor moved quickly to get on top of the situation, appointing a special task force to investigate the charges. [She] deserves credit for dealing with the controversy quickly and forcefully. We're sure UCCS students who serve in the armed forces appreciate the prompt and thorough attention to their concerns."

Not only did Pam act decisively, she immediately followed up with her own written commentary, which was published by both the campus and community newspapers. In it she detailed her actions and thanked the task force, which "found no credible examples of students whose academic progress was damaged by UCCS policies or classroom practices," for its work. In fact, the task force identified multiple instances where faculty and staff assisted students when they were called to military duty. Shockley-Zalabak concluded her article by stating that she was "particularly gratified by the response from current students, alumni, and faculty who came forward in support of deployed students. This is the UCCS spirit that I expect and students deserve."

Shockley-Zalabak understands the importance of organizational communication. Her primary research agenda over the years has revolved around examining communication behavior and its relationship to organizational trust. "An individual will trust you on an interpersonal level if he or she thinks you are open and honest, can identify with you, and believes that you are reliable. The people I interact with determine whether my answers make sense, whether they think I am telling the truth, whether they think I know what I am talking about or not. If they understand me as an individual and my intentions as a leader, then I am credible. However, they won't really trust me as their leader if I am not competent. And, if I am not competent, how can I possibly be considered credible?"

Pam's long history at UCCS, where she has spent her entire academic career, speaks to both her competence and credibility. She began in 1975 as an instructor teaching interpersonal and organizational communication, became department chair in 1980, and then, while continuing to teach, moved rapidly through a series of administrative positions in the 1990s. Beginning in 1992, she transitioned into a new administrative position every two years—coordinator of special projects for the dean of Letters, Arts and Sciences; special assistant to the chancellor for Student Success; dean of the Student Success Initiative/Student Affairs Division; and vice chancellor for Student Success. In 2001 she took over as interim chancellor and was appointed permanently to that position in 2002. As CEO of the University of Colorado at Colorado Springs, Shockley-Zalabak is responsible for an annual budget of $117 million as well as the daily activities of 514 faculty, 392 staff, and more than 7,500 students. During her tenure at UCCS, Pam has earned numerous university and professional awards, including the 2003 Colorado Springs Chamber of Commerce ATHENA Women in Business Award and the 2005 Student Government Association Student Choice for Instructor of the Year Award, and a Telly Award for her role as an executive producer of a television documentary. In addition, she consults for organizations, such as Hewlett-Packard, J. D. Edwards, Bristol-Myers Squibb, USA Cycling, and IRI (Rome, Italy), about organization communication.

"I have stayed at the University of Colorado because I have been able to excel in my academic discipline while at the same time making meaningful contributions to UCCS. I am very, very committed to the University of Colorado. I understand commitment solely to your profession through disciplinary association, but it's a little bit sad. It's empty. I firmly believe that the combination of disciplinary *and* institutional commitments is critical. If you don't care about both, you shouldn't be in them.

"I consider commitment and passion, even loyalty to the institution, when I hire someone. I do hire people for their professional associations, but I expect them to contribute to the University of Colorado as well. I see no conflicts across these venues. Loyal people ultimately change the world a little bit at a time because of their commitment and the work they do for their organization. They put the organization as a high priority in their lives. They often work to bring about change and take risks because of their commitment to something greater than their own careers."

Her own life is testament to the truth of this belief. As a consummate academic, Pam demonstrates a continual dedication to her academic discipline. She has authored six books and more than 100 articles and video productions on communication, trust, and cultures and their influence on overall organizational effectiveness. The insights gained in her academic endeavors directly affect her ability and success as an administrator.

"Communication revolves around information and how you use it. Effective leaders appreciate the process of continual learning—how to access information and evaluate that information. For example, when I took over as chancellor, I did not know how to plan complex organization budgets. I needed to get that knowledge, and I did. Knowledge can be processes or facts and figures, but it can also be an understanding of values—cultural values as well as the values of public higher education. A chief component of competence and credibility has to do with information. If I don't understand values as they relate to my organization or the issues it and higher education in general face, then I don't think I can be competent.

"A great leader constantly listens for and to multiple sources of information. He or she asks, what does this tell me about my organization, its culture, and its workings? And, what do I do with it? Does this information help move us forward in a new direction, confirm important realities, and/or cause us to pause?

"It is hard to see new opportunities and new challenges. I stay current with professional publications and on issues specific to higher education as well as broader societal issues, such as globalization, emerging technology, and sustainability. I read broadly. I frequently listen to a variety of national news and issue forums and learn from the web. I stay in touch with colleagues who work in these areas. Professional associations also provide opportunities for analysis of trends, as does the business community. It's my way of gaining perspective about issues within the context of what we face within the culture of the university.

"Knowledge of the organization's culture makes it possible to better gauge how people will perceive messages about who I am, about change, or about problems. We learn so much when we become good cultural observers. If we don't observe, then we really give way to culture, prior behavior, values, and expectations." She counsels, "Find the answers to questions like: What do I understand about my environment? How am I thinking about my environment? How am I being understood by those in my environment? Ultimately, information and its subsequent understandings need to be communicated, but although being an excellent public speaker is essential, it is one small component of the communicator equation. Effective communicators are those individuals who can encourage, motivate, and lead using information.

"Culling information and blending it with a healthy dose of intuition is both an art and a science that reflects on personal competence. At times, competence comes from those around you and with whom you work. For instance, Colorado's winters are snowy and sometimes treacherous. Living here often requires making decisions about campus closings. I make those decisions, and although I depend heavily on information, I also act on recommendations from the campus chief of police. I don't second-guess him. He knows his business. His competence enhances my credibility.

"I pride myself on being factually orientated and objective. You have to be when leading a large university system—that's the science of decision making. At the same time, intuition has a role to play, and that's the art of it. I made my worst and best decisions both in the same week. In the first instance, on paper it looked like I was making the right decision, but I kept having a reservation, and I didn't listen to it. I hired a person for a student leadership position and he didn't last. He simply didn't value getting things done; rather he 'talked' a lot about getting things done. In the second, there was a person who applied for an important finance administrator position at UCCS who did not have as much experience as the other people in the pool. But this person's action, energy, ideas, and charisma told me he could help me accomplish more than the most experienced applicant. The position required building new levels of community partnerships. I took a chance and hired the person with less experience, and it worked out well.

"The facts and objective realities of an individual's experience are not all that matter in hiring decisions. Your 'gut reaction' that someone can or cannot do the job needs to be factored in as well. If you have a reservation, then you need to be reflective enough to try to understand why it exists. If you don't, you could be making a bad decision. I cannot stress enough the importance of knowing and being able to balance the 'art and the science' of decision making in personnel decisions because it is the people who make all of the difference.

"I do a great deal of postassessment on what works and what didn't go in a particularly good direction. For example, in my leadership team, we take every major success or failure and debrief on what we think worked or what we think failed and why. Recently we announced a major change in benefits. Confusion resulted. We had been accurate in our messages but incomplete in providing individuals with ways to assess the impact on them personally. We had not been comprehensive enough. Debriefs help me think about future approaches to issues.

"I am also an avowed people watcher and probably have been for all of my professional life. I observe people and systems, from children to our entire public higher education administration system. I want to understand what works for people and what doesn't. I am constantly thinking about and planning forward with a focus on a particular outcome and what will help move the organization toward that reality."

As a new chancellor, Pam's move to meet the need for more scholarships illustrates this strategy well. "The number and [dollar] amount of awards needed to increase by a tremendous amount. I set an impossible goal for myself of 300 new privately funded awards. Then, along with others in administration and the foundation, I divided the goal into manageable 'calls' an individual and/or foundation member could make. By sharing the work, we achieved over 400 new awards within three years."

Besides understanding people, she contends that to be effective she must know herself. For instance, "I know that fatigue causes me to take a more cautious, almost paralyzed position on issues. I know I should never, unless it is an absolute necessity, make a serious decision late at night when I'm tired. Other people can make perfect decisions late at night, but I am a morning person, I make great decisions at 7:00 a.m. Everyone must know about his or her own fatigue levels, and they need to stay healthy. I do a tremendous amount of walking on campus, including stairs. I deliberately do not move my car around campus; I walk. I recently started an exercise routine to make sure I am out and moving around. The variability of my schedule makes having a set routine virtually impossible. My days are long. I start between 5:00 and 5:30 in the morning, usually leaving the house no later than 7:00. My average day includes approximately ten meetings, one or two presentations, and an evening event—either an athletic or dinner function. I try to schedule no more than four night functions per week. I typically get home between 7:00 and 10:00 at night." Even so, for mental health and growth, she teaches a graduate class on "emerging communications technology" and an undergraduate class in organizational communication every fall and spring semester.

Pam is close in age to several women featured in this book and, like them, will eventually retire. And her background and upbringing have a familiar ring in terms of when and how she grew up. She was born in Texas in 1944 but moved with her family when she was two years old to Drummond, a town of fewer than 300 people in northwestern Oklahoma. An only child, Pam's father was in the hardware business and, at age thirteen, Pam began keeping the accounts during the busy harvest season. Her mother was a public school teacher who finished her degree before Pam started school. Because there were no day care facilities in Drummond, Pam accompanied her mother to Phillips University, where professors let her sit quietly in class. Early in her school years, Pam announced she did not need to go to college because she had already been. Regardless, her parents always expected her to be a college graduate. In school, Pam was active in sports (basketball, volleyball, and softball) and music. Activities with her church youth group were also important. The highlights of her summer vacations were the times she and her parents spent in Aspen for the music festival and fly-fishing.

In 1975, Pam married a NASA physicist, Charles Zalabak. "Charles and I grew up in Drummond. Our fathers were in business together. We met again after several years of professional work, married, and moved immediately to Colorado so we could both travel from a location we dearly loved." She lost her husband unexpectedly five years ago at about the same time she became chancellor. Speaking of that loss, she says, "Being single in a leadership position is interesting, possible, and difficult. But without doubt, losing my life partner is more difficult than being a 'single' leader. Doing everything alone does present an added set of responsibilities."

Although many of the challenges she and other women of her generation faced when they entered top-level leadership positions have lessened or in some cases disappeared, two persistent issues for women leaders—excessive public scrutiny and personal-professional life balance—concern Pam. "Public scrutiny is something that men are more used to experiencing. Women in the academy need to recognize it and be better able to handle it. A greater challenge for women, more so than scrutiny, is balancing responsibilities within the family and across their personal and professional lives. I married later in my life and in my academic and administrative career. When I did I became a stepmother. Although I did not deal with the challenges of pregnancy and child care concerns, I faced becoming the stepmother of a teen-age daughter, which can be a particularly stressful task. Determining how to balance family and work concerns many women and keeps them from thinking about leadership positions. I worry that we don't have enough women wanting to take positions above the dean's level, even though I think opportunities for women in higher education today are extraordinary. In the University of Colorado System, for instance, the applicant pools across the system include fewer women than they have in the past.

"Although the retiree exodus from administrative positions across the board that we are or will experience shortly represents a great loss for higher education leadership, it does provide a wide range of opportunities for women at all levels. We need new strategies to generate change in the twenty-first-century university—for everything from funding, to curriculum, to energizing students of the future, to dealing with the gender (and minority) gaps in science and technology. And women need to see themselves leading this change, along with their male counterparts.

"Women have to be able to balance responsibilities and create priorities that allow them to feel effective at home and work. Fortunately for me, throughout our years together and in the early years when Yvonne lived with us, both Charles and Yvonne were supportive of my needs as an administrator. We all shared the work of living together. I know we can find a way to make it work. I absolutely want there to be more women deans, vice chancellors, presidents, and chancellors."

She warns, however, that women (and men) must "be very clear about not wanting to take a position, but wanting to do something about which they care. A title, in a position, without passion is worthless. People make a real mistake when they want a title of leadership, versus [asking themselves,] what do I want to accomplish with this leadership?" Pam models her passion and commitment across her life's interests and currently as a grandmother, university system chancellor, organizational communications academic researcher, and longtime resident of Colorado and Oklahoma.

Each of these venues has influenced who she is, what she does, and where she is going. Today, her stepdaughter, son-in-law, and granddaughter are a "special part of her life." Yvonne, Carissa, and Pam were recently on safari in Africa. At least four times a year they spend time together. Pam travels to California for middle school softball and basketball and cheers her granddaughter from the sidelines. She remains a music lover and values her time in the Colorado mountains and at the family farm in Oklahoma. At the University of Colorado, credibility and competence, trust in people, and a focus on communication permeate her actions, decisions, and direction. Her success in life and in leadership is based on a balance of what she values at home and at work.

BIBLIOGRAPHIC NOTES

Pamela Sue Shockley-Zalabak's story derives from multiple sources, including interview transcripts; vitae; a brief family profile; University of Colorado, Colorado Springs, websites; articles by Ron Fitz, Colorado Springs reporter for the University of Colorado *Silver and Gold Record* (August 25, 2005; February 2, 2006; April 20, 2006; July 6, 2006; August 17, 2006; December 7, 2006; December 21, 2006); articles from the online edition of the *Colorado Springs Gazette* by Amanda Mountain (April 25, 2005), Brian Newsome (October 31, 2006; December 26, 2006), and others (February 3, 2006; October 19, 2006), including Pamela Shockley-Zalabak, "Supporting the Military Still a Priority at UCCS" (October 18, 2006); "Chamber Receives Chancellor's Award," *Colorado Springs Business Journal* (June 9, 2006); and "Emmer Leading Ent to Prominence in City, State" (December 22, 2006).

NINE

LOVING THE PRESIDENCY

Betty L. Siegel
Kennesaw State University

THE LIFE AND CAREER of Dr. Betty, or Miss Betty, as she is known at the local Waffle House, has become the stuff of legend and stories. Upon the announcement of her retirement from the presidency, Georgia Senator Johnny Isakson remarked on the U.S. Senate floor, "It gives me a great deal of pleasure to recognize the contributions of Dr. Betty Siegel to the children of Georgia, her contributions to higher education, the ceiling she broke for women in academics in our State, and, most importantly, her continuing [commitment] to helping and teaching our young people." The chancellor of the University System of Georgia called her "an icon among American college presidents." Another icon, Coca-Cola, honored her career with a special edition Coke bottle distributed at her retirement banquet. As the longest-serving woman president of an American public higher education institution, Dr. Betty Siegel blazed a trail for women leaders in higher education.

Betty Siegel was the first woman to lead a Georgia public college. In doing so, she transformed Kennesaw College from a small commuter college to the third-largest university in the

University System of Georgia. During a recent Georgia Public Broadcasting interview, she commented, "I was intrigued by that little college. It was the early 1980s and the focus was on the growth in the Sunbelt. The thought was that the universities that would flourish in the future would be close to major growth areas and economic thoroughfares. And they would be for nontraditional students. The minute I saw Kennesaw I thought, my gosh, this is a prototype.

"I wanted [Kennesaw] to be a college of meaning. I wanted it to be more than a collection of courses, to be more than a drive-in college. I didn't want our students to come and just have an in-class experience. I wanted them to have a total experience. I wanted them to have life-changing experiences. When I came in 1981, we had 3,738 students. By 2006, we had close to 19,000. Early on, we didn't have diversity in our student body; only 7% of our students were minorities. Today 20% are minority, and we have 1,600 students from 132 countries on our campus. What a difference! We're an international university, growing in size, stature, selectivity, specialization, and significance.

"I've been president at Kennesaw [KSU] for twenty-five years. During that time I have led five different kinds of institutions. I had to change just as the institution had to change. In any job one has to be moving, fluid, adjusting, reconsidering, rethinking, perhaps, reinforcing. Gail Godwin commented in *The Finishing School* that either you congeal and reach your final form by about eighteen, or you make new trysts with life. As a developmental psychologist, I've always felt it was better to make new trysts, to grow into new dimensions I never thought of before. To be congealed would be so awful.

"When I look at what we did here at Kennesaw, it's an exercise in change. We were profiled in *Searching for Academic Excellence: Twenty Colleges and Universities on the Move and Their Leaders*. The thesis of the book was that the perspective of the president is very important. Some universities need a fixer. Others need an athletic coach. Still others require an accountant. Some people take one dimension and that's their one note. That's why I think presidents move on. They've done their old Johnny One-Note. And that's fine. I choose to think that's too limited. There are many dimensions of the presidency, and these times need many perspectives from the president. I've grown and stayed for a quarter of a century. It's unusual. In fact, I'm participating in an ACE [American Council on Education] study on the sustained presidency.

"When Howard Gardner wrote *Leading Minds*, he said leaders must tell their stories. That freed me. I grew up in the mountains of Kentucky. Mountain people are storytellers. As children we sat listening to elders telling our history through stories. My grandfather used to sit in a swing on the porch. That swing is now on my porch and it must be 150 years old. He'd say, 'Come sit a spell.' And he'd share stories. I love storytelling. I enjoy speechmaking. Even though, you're disclosing and you're very vulnerable when you're speaking, I chose to take the role of storyteller.

"I like public forums and opportunities where authenticity can shine through and I can share my vision. I'm comfortable walking around, engaging people. I want to let them know that I covet their attention, covet their ideas. There are different ways to do it. For example, if I am giving a commencement speech, I don't use notes. It makes me struggle to signal what I need to say. I may have three or four quotes written down and that's it. It works for me. Years ago I asked Arthur Combs, a friend at the University of Florida, 'How long did it take you to write that speech?' He said, 'About eighteen years. Finally got it right.' I asked, 'How many speeches do you have?' He pulled six index cards out of his pocket and said, 'I have five good ones. The other one is for backup.' That's my style, too.

"The key is to tell *your* story. You cannot tell somebody else's story. I had a friend who liked one of my stories and memorized it word for word and then substituted her name on it. I found out about it. The story was what I learned about cheating in the fourth grade. It is a very painful story that always brings tears to my eyes. I told her, 'You can't do that. It's my story.' She said, 'Oh, but it's such a good story.' I replied, 'But when you tell it, it's not true. You cannot tell it the same way I tell it. You must be authentic.

"The ability to communicate is an important skill. I believe very strongly, as Warren Bennis says, that leaders are those who enroll others in their vision. You must communicate well to do that. As a leader you must be an inviter who says to others, 'Come walk with me. Just walk. Let's talk together. Let's explore together in an atmosphere of trust.' Leaders must find their best way to communicate. If you can communicate only in small groups, do it till you drop. If you can only do it from the platform, then make it a bully pulpit. If you can't do that, then communicate with your team. Find a way to write. You must communicate because you're 'enrolling others in your vision.' I spent twelve nights in campus housing sleeping over with students. I sat up all night playing cards, watching television, and talking. Students also came by my office regularly, and faculty too. I set in place a lot of leadership programs for faculty, staff, students, and administrators.

"There is a little Waffle House on the side of the campus. For years I've been going there. I go every day. I sit at the same table, and when I walk in it's ready for me. I read three newspapers— the *Marion Daily Journal* to understand the county, the *Atlanta Journal* to understand the state, and the *New York Times*. Then I put the papers aside so people can come over and talk and visit with me. I had meetings with students there, and I'd take notes on the Waffle House napkins. Sometimes students told me about a teacher they liked. I sent a letter to that teacher, saying, 'Somebody told me that you were a really great teacher for these reasons. Take this letter and give it to the Waffle House. Free breakfast on me.' Once I sat at the Waffle House for three hours free-associating with someone. I wrote twenty-four napkins full of ideas that started Kennesaw on the Year of Service, which was followed by the Year of Engagement, then the Year of Collaboration, then the Year of Success. So we have a theme every year. And it started at the Waffle House.

"The Waffle House has adopted me." At her retirement, Betty received a "Golden Waffle Award" from the national headquarters for being such a goodwill ambassador for the restaurant chain, along with free breakfast for a year and a year's worth of certificates to share with others. In February 2007, the Waffle House she frequented as president dedicated her favorite spot with a plaque, which reads "Miss Betty's Booth."

When asked why she liked the Waffle House so much, Betty said when she was small, "we lived in a very small house with no central heat. My mother got up early in the morning, lit the kitchen fire in the wood stove, and put my sister's and my clothes on chairs to warm before the fire because it was so cold. We didn't have a kitchen table. All we had was this little white counter. So we sat at the counter and read while Mother cooked. When I'm at the Waffle House and I'm reading at the table and I can hear them cooking, I associate it with those feelings of warmth and family."

In *Becoming an Invitational Leader,* Betty and co-author William Purkey lay out a framework that guides her actions and the manner in which she communicates. "We talk about four pillars of ethical behavior—respect, trust, optimism, and intentionality."

Working within this framework, leadership "becomes a *mutual* commitment between colleagues. Respect is measured by how we treat ourselves and others. Trust encourages collaborative risk taking and creative problem solving. Optimism is evidenced by positive and realistic expectations. Intentionality gives direction and purpose to our decisions and makes action possible. We call this an ethical theory of practice. The invitational leader uses people, place, policies, programs, and processes (the five Ps) to bring an institution into alignment. Only when they are in sync do you have a truly inviting institution."

The concept of positional power has no place in Betty's invitational leadership style. "I don't even like the word. It's not helpful. Power is not in a position. Now, there is a lot that goes with the position of president. I *can* make things happen. But those things are minute compared to what can be done through personal power. To me, personal power is Cyrano de Bergerac's 'white plume' of leadership, the authenticity of the leader, the attitudes, beliefs, and values to which you hold true. We ought to aspire to that, not to power. The perks of power leave with the job. The personal power you develop doesn't leave you."

Betty believes that the president is not alone in leading the institution. "Building the team is probably one of the most important things a president does. You have to rely on each other, on the team. A new president might think, 'How am I ever going to learn all this? I can't learn all this.' No, you can't; you have to focus on what you do best and what you bring to the job. You build a team based on what each individual can bring to the table, how they complement each other and work with each other. The president cannot be the best at everything; that'd be foolish. No one likes or wants to work with Miss or Mr. Know-It-All. I prefer to admit that I need help. Let's work together. Tell me what you would do. Can we do this? Or that? Let's ask some important questions. Let's have courageous conversations. Those are the things that are important.

"In addition, you can work through conflicts with the right team. When you make changes, you create conflict. I learned somewhere that the first year you are in the presidency you make a decision and 90% love it, 10% hate it. Next year, you make a decision 90% love and 10% hate, but it's a different 10%. So if you stay in the job ten years, you'll make everyone mad at least once. It just goes with the job, but a good team that pulls together makes a president's life easier.

"Good teams also free leaders to be boundary monitors. Leaders must go to the boundary, see what's there, bring it back, and say, 'Look at what I've seen. Does it have some merit for what we're doing? Is it something we might want to emulate? Is it something we want to avoid?' Exploration is very much a part of leadership, and the leader has to be the one who monitors broadly and deeply.

"As a boundary monitor I constantly said to our faculty and staff, 'Listen to these voices, these outside voices.' Over the years the outside voices we've had have been remarkable—Ernest Boyer, Donald Shön, Howard Gardner, Art Levine, George Kuh, Parker Palmer, Lee Schulman, Alexander Astin, Millard Fuller of Habitat for Humanity, Frances Hesselbein. John Gardner came every two years because we were growing so much that I wanted every new freshman professor to have a course with him. These are people I have picked to come, by design, to give voice to different ideas.

"As president you have to be a futurist. You have to skate to where the puck will be, as Gretzky said. You have to read broadly, be a constant student of change. Not just in education, but in sociology, psychology, and human behavior as well. This is what makes the job so interesting." During Betty's twenty-five years as president at Kennesaw, the university expanded its offerings from fifteen baccalaureate-degree programs to fifty-five undergraduate and graduate degree programs. Along the way the institution was cited for excellence in several reports and publications, including recognition by *U.S. News and World Report* in 1989, 1990, and 1991 as a "rising star" Southern institution. In 2003, the American Association of State Colleges and Universities included Kennesaw as one of the first institutions in its Foundations of Excellence in the First College Year program. And in 2008, Kennesaw's first-year experience program was recognized for the third time by *U.S. News and World Report* as one of the top programs in the country.

In 2006, Siegel transitioned from her presidency into a new role as distinguished chair of the KSU Siegel Institute for Leadership, Ethics, and Character. A second institute on ethical leadership was named for her in 2007 in Shanghai, China. Through the institutes she continues to work internationally with leaders in education and other fields to establish programs in social responsibility and global ethical leadership. She also directs the annual Oxford Conclave on Global Ethics, which she launched in 2005, and in 2007 she spent three months in South Africa at Stellenbosch University as a consultant on ethical leadership, student success, and community engagement. "I tell people I am in the third act of my life, first scene—generativity, as Maslow would call it. I am *so* in love with what I am doing now with the Siegel Institute. There is definitely life after retirement.

"At this stage of my life, I am doing a lot of reflecting. One has to own what seems to have worked for you and what you are. I've been thinking about *The Reflective Practitioner* by Donald Shön. He was on our campus early in my career, and I identified very strongly with his work. I also identified with the work of Sidney Jourard. He was a young professor at the University of

Florida when I was there as a young professor. He wrote a book, called *Self-Disclosure*, in which he said that you have to disclose, to be the transparent self. Reflecting and remembering are critical aspects of leadership and learning.

"About three years ago, I read *Remembrance Rock* by Carl Sandburg. He suggested that you should go to the Remembrance Rock and sit on the rock for a day and ask questions: Who am I? Where do I come from? And where am I going? When I was talking with my minister about this, she commented, 'You know, you should ask a fourth question: What is the meaning?' I thought about that and added a fifth question, How do I matter? Two years ago, we placed a huge thirty-ton rock on our campus. At commencement the graduating students received a little piece of rock tied in the school colors from that big rock. The message on it said: Who am I? Where do I come from? Where am I going? What is the meaning? And how do I matter? And it was signed by me. All the students who graduated were supposed to walk by after commencement, put their hands on the rock, and reflect on those questions.

"Presidents must have an emotional Remembrance Rock that prompts them to ask repeatedly, Where am I going? What am I doing? What is the meaning of what I do? And who am I? Where do I come from? How do I own my roots? How do I use my roots to express who I am, what I learned from my roots? And, finally, How do I matter? The most significant thing is to live a life of meaning. If you think only in terms of self-gratification or self-aggrandizement or a position, I think that is sad. And it certainly is not what I want to do as a leader.

"Leaders should always be in a posture of reflecting. Asking themselves, What can I learn from that situation? Was I worthy enough? Did I give my best efforts? Where could I have done better? I don't mean to be constantly looking back but learning from some of our experiences, making improvements and adjustments. For example, I'm generally pretty even-keeled, but once I was having a bad day. And like any bad day, things weren't going well. For some reason that day I was a little bit unbridled, acting 'Oh, poor me.' The next day I wore the same clothes to work again. Clean underwear, of course. And I said to the staff, 'The better Betty is back.' Everybody died laughing; they got it: the better Betty. You see, reflection is the better Betty. I was showing them that I realized I wasn't at my best the day before. I was doing the best I could at the moment. But you know what? I'm better than that. So let me bring back the better Betty."

The hardy, positive attitude of "the better Betty" springs from the upbringing of the child, Betty Faye Lentz. "It is important to 'own our roots as leaders.' Robert Coles in his *Children of Crisis* series said that mountain children are remarkably tenacious in spirit and healthy in mind, and, of course, I choose to believe that. I think the values of the Scotch-Irish who settled in Appalachia were those that honored work and the dignity of the person. It didn't matter what you owned. It mattered who you were. I'm Scotch-Irish from an old Cumberland, Kentucky, family. I was a coal miner's daughter. I elected very early in my career to own that I was a coal miner's daughter. I really believe adversity shapes you, that you can triumph with all kinds of deficits in your life."

Betty has seen rewards for the tenacity of mountain spirit. "My grandfather was killed when my dad was six years old. My mother and father eloped in high school. They never had a day of college. My sister and I were born during the first two years of their marriage. We were very poor. Over the years, my father went from working in the mines to owning them. He went bankrupt when I was in my senior year of high school and lost all his money. But he came back and my parents ended up owning other mines. Our family still owns them, and recently we discovered oil and gas on our land. Isn't that amazing? After all these years, we have this potential!"

Although neither of Betty's parents attended college, her love of education is a tradition of the women in her family. "The men went to work in the mines or to work the land and the women were the ones who really loved education. I remember, when I was in the first grade, I went to school in this little mountain community and sitting on the stage were my mother, grandmother, and great grandmother. They invited me to come up and sit with them. They were being honored for their love of education. I remember swinging my legs and looking around in that gym and thinking, 'This is something.' Just look at these women and what they had meant to education in this little community." As she puts it, "Education was our only window to the world."

Recognition of the value of education has continued in Betty's family. Both she and her younger sister not only graduated from college but have earned their doctorates. "We're both psychologists. My sister, Ella Mae Shearon, founder and director of the Institute of Psychodrama in Cologne, Germany, is probably, very honestly, the world's best psychodramatist." Betty's two sons, Michael and David, are both college professors at Suffolk University and East Carolina University, respectively. Her husband, "life partner in family, in learning, and in service" of over forty years, Joel Siegel, who received his doctorate from Indiana University, recently retired from the professorate in English at Piedmont College, but he continues to serve as associate magistrate court judge for the City of Kennesaw.

Like many of the women whose stories are told in this book, Betty Siegel's career is a collection of firsts. "I was hired by the University of Florida in 1967, the only woman in a department of about thirty men. They didn't want a woman and I showed up five and a half months pregnant! The men had a fit. The dean and my department head were furious that I had not told them I was pregnant. I understand they had never had a pregnant professor at the University of Florida before I arrived. I was to teach human growth and development. Interesting, huh? I don't know what possessed me, but I told those men I'd have the baby during the quarter break and not to worry about a thing; it was going to be okay. They died; the men just couldn't believe me. Well, I finished my last exam, went out to eat and shop with my husband. We went to a movie and I went into labor that evening and had the baby the next morning. My husband brought the exams to the hospital. I graded them and I got them turned in before any of the men did. I had the baby and didn't miss class, didn't miss an hour, didn't miss a meeting, nothing. This is the stuff of legend now. It seemed that everyone on campus knew what had happened, so at the University of Florida I became known as 'that woman.'" Several years later, Betty received the first University of Florida Distinguished Teacher of the Year award. In 1971, she became the university's first woman dean, a distinction she also held at Western Carolina University.

Thanks to the trailblazing courage of the women leaders of Betty Siegel's generation, "women are coming into new positions of authority and coming into positions of authority in larger numbers than before. But we still have further to go. I don't know why I've been so successful. I've never used being a woman as an explanation for why I didn't get something. But I know I've not gotten some things because I was a woman. I interviewed for a job once and no one knew that one of my friends was a member of the search committee. She told me afterward that some of the committee members said, 'If that candidate had been a man, we'd have hired him on the spot.' I just laugh at that kind of thinking. That's their problem; it's not mine.

"I think women have to get past any possible prejudice and find ways in which they become integral to the organizations they want to serve. How do you do it? I can't give you a prescription, but I think it's how you use who you are and what you do. It's getting beyond the fact that some doors are closed.

"Women do have to concentrate on the career dimension of their lives. But they must be careful what they swap for it. You have to give a lot to make it to the top and do well. Young women today think they can have it all, and they're destined not to have it all. Nobody says you've got to have it all. Sometimes one needs to be sanguine, be more accepting, less driven. I have a whole speech I give, called "That ought to be enough." In it I ask, what is it that's enough? How many more things do you need? What needs to be enough? For me it's been worth it. I love it! I just loved being president. But sometimes I think I should've spent more time in play. My boys tell me that we played well; we talked well; we're fine. But maybe I should have paid more attention to self. Still, I have no regrets.

"I read recently something that was attributed to the chaplain at Harvard. He said you can have a job, you can have a career, or you can have a calling. I've never thought of the presidency as anything but a calling. If you're called and you accept the commitment, you have to be very excited by it, passionate about it, feel called to do it. Otherwise, you should 'get out of Dodge.'

"I believe in having a passion in life. Passion spills out into one's personal and professional life. I have passion about my work, passion about my family, passion about my country. I'm passionate about authenticity, passionate about the arts. People exhibit passion in many different ways, consciously and unconsciously. I think part of passion is being an avid learner, to be extraordinarily interested in things, particularly in new things, seeking out new adventures, new opportunities. Passion implies leaning in to what is life and savoring it. I think my passion is evident in my work. I feel as energized today after twenty-five years as I did when I began. I've never been more excited in my life than I am right now. Leadership is not a job. It's not a position. It is passion for one's work. Maslow, whom I quote often, said that true creativity is work that goes someplace joyfully. So to me, passion has to be a part of that going someplace joyfully. One must feel strongly. It must be very sad indeed to be lukewarm."

William Purkey said of Betty Siegel, "If I had to sum it up with one statement, I think it would be that Betty's passion for living, learning, and leading is contagious. She is truly a beneficial presence in the lives of countless individuals." In tribute to Betty's commitment to ethical leadership, several experts on leadership, including Frances Hesselbein, Howard Gardner, and John Hume, dedicated the book, *For the Common Good: The Ethics of Leadership in the 21st Century*, to her, saying, "When the significant American educational leaders of the last quarter century are listed, Betty Siegel will be in that select company."

A plaque in Betty Siegel's conference room highlights a quote from Ralph Waldo Emerson, "Do not go where the path may lead. Go instead where there is no path and leave a trail." Advice she has certainly heeded.

BIBLIOGRAPHICAL NOTES

The chapter on Betty Siegel was crafted through personal interviews with Siegel as well as several of her presentations; interviews conducted by Georgia Public Broadcasting and the

Turknett Leadership Group; Kennesaw State University and Siegel Institute for Leadership websites; William Purkey & Betty Siegel, *Becoming an Invitational Leader* (Lake Worth, FL: Humanics Trade Group, 2002); and John C. Knapp (Ed.), *For the Common Good: The Ethics of Leadership in the 21st Century* (Westport, CT: Praeger, 2006).

TEN

GIVING BACK

Karen Gayton Swisher
Haskell Indian Nations University

Y OU CANNOT UNDERSTAND Karen Swisher as a leader unless you understand her strong ties to her tribal community,
family, and the institution she served. They inexplicably inter-
twine to produce a subtly complex individual—quiet, dedicated,
spiritually grounded, optimistic, and caring. She clearly articulated these ties when she described the most defining moment
of her career.

"In addition to the births of my son and daughter, and my two
granddaughters, it was when my tribe supported my inauguration as president of Haskell. They not only paid for the whole
event, they sent a busload of adults and students to participate in
the activities. It fully demonstrated a contradiction to what many
people say about educated native people—that you can't go home
again or that you are not accepted if you become too well
educated.

"I have never been quite sure why people think I am a leader.
I am always surprised when chosen. Even so, early on I learned
some important things about myself. I am part of a very small
'N,' Native American female. I love teaching. I am creative. I can

get my point across when I want to. Diversity is positive if you want it to be. The reservation experience is valuable in the whole scheme of things. And, although I chose a profession, teaching, that is typically and traditionally female, I ended up in administration, which is still a man's world; and I learned I not only could hold my own, but that I could excel."

Karen Gayton Swisher was born in 1943 and raised on the Standing Rock Sioux Reservation in North Dakota. Her father, a Sioux tribal member, began his education at a Catholic boarding school and ended it at about the eighth grade at a government boarding school in Flandreau, South Dakota. He was a farmer/ rancher. "I never knew that he wasn't 'educated' because he knew all he needed to know about his cattle and farming. My mother (originally from Minnesota) attended a normal school and then moved to Sioux County to teach. She later became the county superintendent of schools, altogether working over forty-five years in Sioux County. My older brothers continued their education beyond high school, but I am the only one in my immediate family to have completed a four-year degree.

"Although I don't recall ever explicitly hearing it, I think my parents and my brothers expected me to go to college, and I wanted to. Certainly, my mother was an influence on my wanting to be a teacher. And, my dad got me to think about a life off the reservation. He wanted me to have more opportunities than he saw on the reservation at that time.

"Life on the reservation actually prepared me for moving away. I grew up with lots of cousins. My father had four brothers and five sisters and my mother had a brother. We cousins spent time together in the summer. And during the school year, I stayed in town with friends and cousins as often as I could because it was much more fun than being home out in the country with no one to play with. I was quite a bum." When Karen left for college,

Northern State Teachers College in Aberdeen, South Dakota, seemed a logical choice for her because she had two uncles living there.

"I was prepared emotionally for college and I thought I was prepared academically (I was valedictorian), but I found out that an A at Fort Yates High School did not translate into an A at college. I had to work harder. College on-campus social support is extremely important for Native students. For us, it was Evelyn Bergen, the higher education liaison at the BIA [Bureau of Indian Affairs] Area Office in Aberdeen. She was a cultured woman, in both the mainstream and the native world, from the Rosebud reservation. So she not only understood our backgrounds, but she knew how to succeed in the mainstream world. We also had a club, called Moccasin Tracks, an early version of Native American student campus organizations, that provided a strong support system all four years of college.

"When I graduated, the best teachers' salaries were in Minnesota, and I had family in Minneapolis, so I took a job in Bloomington teaching second grade. I stayed with my mom's cousin and her daughter who was my age. Again, family played an important part in my life's decisions. A year later I married, and after short stays in South Dakota and New York, we returned to Standing Rock, where I worked until my family and I moved off-reservation."

During more than twenty-five years away from the reservation, Karen's tribal values, "especially those that speak of loyalty, humility, bravery, fortitude, wisdom, and generosity," provided the same cultural blueprint for her that many Indian people carry with them. "Native Americans who have lived in urban settings for generations still maintain ties to their reservations, coming back and giving back. These values and the actions they inspire guide my life and keep it in balance.

"Culture shapes the way we lead. In many Indian cultures, it's what somebody else says about you that counts. For Native Americans, there is a reluctance to say what you do, what you've contributed. And, I share that reluctance. In fact, I'm too hard on myself. Even now that I'm at the end of my career and I know I've done a lot of things, I immediately flip to what I could've or should've done."

During her time at Haskell, it was difficult for her to be the most visible person on campus. "Being in the spotlight, and getting all of the attention, was sometimes bothersome to me because I knew that in reality there are many other people who make Haskell run. I've battled this inability to self-promote (a requisite of the dominant White culture in which we live) all of my life."

"Giving back" drives much of what Karen does. "I came to Haskell because I thought I could contribute to something significant and be in a place where everyone knows the mission and knows why we are here. Its institutional values—responsibility, respect, cooperation, and honesty—coincide with mine. And I strongly believe in Haskell's vision of 'empowering American Indians and Alaskan Native scholars for leadership and service to sovereign first nations and the world.' It gives me great pride to know that what was once an institution that prepared young Indian people for assimilation is now an institution of the federal government that prepares young people to be leaders in indigenous self-determination, and that I played a role in its transformation."

Haskell Indian Nations University's story mirrors that of the tribes/nations it serves. It is one of endurance and survival. Haskell, the oldest tribal college in the country, opened in 1884 as an industrial training boarding school under the auspices of the Bureau of Indian Affairs, providing agricultural education for its young Indian students. Its sole purpose was to hasten its students' assimilation into the European lifestyle of mainstream America.

Haskell is one of only two tribal colleges funded entirely by the federal government and the only one to have evolved into a four-year university. It is also the only tribal college whose enrollment is 100% American Indian/Alaska Native and intertribal, with students from more than 140 tribes/nations, although almost 50% of them come from Oklahoma and Kansas, close to Haskell's 320-acre campus in Lawrence, Kansas. Two-thirds of its entering students are not academically ready for college work in math or English, and one-third require remedial work in both areas. Even so, almost one-half of Haskell's four-year degree graduates go on to law or graduate school and do well.

"As part of its fulfillment of provisions in over 100 treaties signed between 1794 and 1871 to provide education for Indian children, the federal government funds Haskell. Unlike Gallaudet or Howard universities, whose budgets are line items, a provision that allows them to negotiate directly with Congress, Haskell's funding is subsumed within the BIA budget under the Department of the Interior. The monies Congress authorizes guarantee that students can attend tuition-free and receive on-campus room and board at minimal cost. These allocations carry stipulations that limit the number of semesters students can attend at no charge, six and twelve semesters for two-year and four-year degrees, respectively." This limitation, coupled with academic unpreparedness, negatively affects graduation rates and subjects the institution to constant government scrutiny.

Haskell became a fully accredited junior college in the 1970s and by the 1990s had moved away from its assimilation charge to one that openly embraces cultural traditions. In 1993, Haskell offered its first baccalaureate degree; vocational education programs were phased out; and the institution changed its name to Haskell Indian Nations University. In 1998, it added three more bachelor's degrees to its offerings.

Today, Haskell serves 900 students and has about 210 employees with an operational budget of approximately $9.5 million and an additional $3.8 million for facilities management. In addition, it receives approximately $1.5 million for sponsored programs. As of 2004 its program budget had not increased in ten years. Much of Swisher's tenure as president was spent dealing with budgetary shortfalls.

"My first real encounter with Haskell came in 1993, when I served as a member of a national group of Indian educators that reworked an earlier four-year teacher education proposal to make the curriculum more culturally appropriate. We share an identity as Indians but carry diversity of cultural backgrounds, traditional and nontraditional, and community structure—reservation, small villages, rural, suburban, and urban communities where Native cultures are barely visible. As a consequence, culture here can be defined on at least three levels: spiritual (there's a Greater Being over all of us), social (how we interact—there's generosity of sharing and giving here), and intellectual (students are actually learning about culture and its impact)."

The extent of Haskell's culturally based curriculum is unparalleled in higher education. It builds on the creative and cultural traditions of leadership and service, emphasizing sovereignty, self-determination, and holistic learning approaches. Haskell's bachelor's degrees—American Indian studies, business administration, elementary education, and environmental science (tribal lands issues)—reflect tribal community leadership needs as do many of its associate degrees. Each baccalaureate program includes a service component, which reinforces the expectation that students and graduates honor their debts to their ancestors by serving as role models for or working in their tribal communities, and in society in general.

In 1994, Karen returned to Haskell on an Intergovernmental Personnel Act Agreement between Arizona State University (ASU) (state government) and Haskell (federal) for six months to help prepare the campus for accreditation review by the Kansas State Board of Education. She moved permanently to Haskell in1996 as chair of the teacher education department. In 1998, she became dean of instruction, then interim president in 1999, and, finally, president in 2000. In early 2007, she retired, leaving behind a quiet but substantial legacy.

Swisher was Haskell's fourth president and the first woman to serve in that role. Earlier she taught at Arizona State University and the University of Utah for a combined fourteen years. She began her gradual climb to the presidency as an elementary principal of a BIA school in North Dakota, a job she loved. "When my husband and I moved to Huron, South Dakota, I decided not to go back to the classroom because I was not as compelled to work in a place where the purpose was not so well defined for me as it had been back on the reservation. Instead, I entered an educational leadership doctoral program on a two-year fellowship at the University of North Dakota. In hindsight, two years was definitely not enough time to savor the ideal world of theories and gaining new knowledge."

Throughout her career she has tried to prepare herself both mentally and emotionally for what she needed to do. Even so, "When I became president I didn't know how to be a president. I didn't have a feel for the long hours—the very magnitude of the responsibility of the job is unbelievable. I took over in July, and in August four students died in an auto accident. Three of them were our students. Then the Haskell Foundation collapsed in December when it was discovered that the former director had embezzled over $100,000. And the Haskell-Baker Wetlands highway issue reared its ugly head again." With the Kansas Department of Transportation advocating building through the wetlands, and university and environmental groups opposing it, this fifteen-year-old controversy, once thought resolved, continues to the present. "That was quite an introduction to the presidency."

Over the years, she became more confident about being the president instead of, as she put it, "just doing the job." She explained, "When I'm out in a visible leadership situation, whether on campus or not, then I'm the president. But when I'm sitting at my computer answering the hundreds of e-mails and phone calls that I get, I'm doing the job. The presidency is leadership with a task, management.

"I've always been passionate about Indian education, and as a teacher or leader I've always been passionate about what I was doing, or else I wouldn't do it. But, I didn't have to be as passionate about other jobs as I did as Haskell's president. Comparatively speaking, I had to show more outward passion for this job than I did for any other job, but that was easy because I loved my job. My professional life as president was my personal life. I didn't have a family to care for because I had been divorced since 1990, and my children were grown. So I attended every student event I could because I had the time."

Two of her most lasting achievements as president—taking the campus through strategic planning and the successful ten-year continued accreditation of the institution in 2005 as a result of the strategic planning—are also ones that she is most proud of. "Using a strategic planning process, Haskell employees were asked what's working and what's not. The end result was a fourteen-page list, only one page of which featured what was working at Haskell. The remaining thirteen pages highlighted thirty trouble spots. We identified some of the most crucial concerns as communication and decision making, professional development, and funding.

"It seemed that decisions weren't made about some things, improper decisions were made about others, and no one really knew who made the decisions. To improve the situation, I expanded the President's Council. Originally its membership was limited to the president, the dean of instruction, the dean of student services, the facilities manager, and the administrative officer. I immediately added the Faculty Senate and Student Senate presidents. By 2003, the Council included union and support staff representatives, deans, and the directors of athletics and Title III programs and had changed its name to the University Council. As a result, decision making became more participatory and transparent and communication across campus improved, although after seven years we still talk about communication problems. In some respects, the situation is complicated by the fact that Haskell has had difficulty embracing the notion of shared governance so typical on most university campuses, perhaps because its employees are federal, not state or tribal, and the institution has historically operated as a top-down federal bureaucracy."

Professional development for faculty, staff, and students, including leadership development, was important to Karen during her presidency. "I sponsored study groups around readings on leadership so that administrators were speaking the same language. I encouraged others to think about their own style of leadership and to further their education when I saw the potential of a good, strong administrator. We need to prepare people for leadership. I didn't have enough people taking initiative within their positions; maybe it's the government involvement. People here waited for me to come up with the ideas. They equated it to being the president, to providing leadership. It was energy draining for me. I should have been saying, 'Let me give you the endorsement' rather than providing all of the ideas. Seeing others develop as leaders gives me great pleasure. I like it when someone else takes the spotlight. I get a big charge out of it.

"Funding, however, is the most pervasive issue that Haskell faces. In the last five years, overall increases have not been sufficient to cover existing personnel and cost of living increases. To compensate, we had to make the difficult decision to direct money away from programming or not fill vacancies and retirements to make up the difference. In all, Haskell has suffered a five-year cumulative decrease of nearly 40% in program expenditures. Thirty percent of its full-time faculty slots are vacant. For the first time, Haskell is considering opening the culturally based classes to tuition-paying, non-Indian students to help raise funds to sustain programs and cover other university operations. In addition, the university set a strategic goal of raising $20 million, which I think is doable. It will be difficult, though, because current federal ethics rules prohibit Haskell personnel from requesting additional funds from Congress, and the rules are not clear about directly soliciting funds from Indian Nations."

In her ten years at Haskell, Karen dealt with big issues—curricular, financial, moving the institution from a community college to a baccalaureate institution. But, she didn't overlook the seemingly small issues that symbolically make a huge difference. "I cleaned up and beautified the campus, recognizing that aesthetics are important. Now the campus community and alumni take pride in their surroundings. And my door was always open. Most meaningful to me when I left the presidency was to hear maintenance and facilities people say they appreciated my accessibility.

"Over the years, I learned that it can be lonely at the top, especially for women administrators. When you deal with problems of the magnitude that Haskell faces, you need to hear unbiased opinions from knowledgeable people who can help you think through the options. I depended on a cadre of tribal college presidents who served as my primary support network and confidants. My academic vice president also served that role in the last two years. It was good for her upward mobility to learn what it's like at the top. In addition, through my involvement with the American Council on Education minority and women in higher education commissions, I met many women presidents of color who had similar experiences. And I had several male friends who have been there for me. The two male past presidents of Haskell, in particular, were very helpful any time I asked for their opinions or ideas.

"Unlike many women, over the course of my career, I was truly blessed with few incidents of discrimination. Even though I am shy and sometimes lack confidence, I realize that I never viewed myself as a victim because of my gender or ethnicity. I grew up with a very healthy sense of who I am—that I am Indian, Norwegian, English, and Irish. Perhaps because I am not as dark-skinned as some, I didn't suffer discrimination because of the color of my skin."

Her Native American heritage has had an impact, however, on the way in which she conducts herself. "I didn't want anyone making excuses for me or feeling sorry for me because I was from the reservation. I had one chance to get it right, so I played new experiences through in my head. I tried to anticipate what would be expected, and, when possible, I observed before participating. Because I am an Indian woman, I felt that I needed to be a role model."

Although Karen escaped race-based prejudicial treatment, she has led a life influenced, at least in part, by gender expectations. "As seniors in high school, all the girls were told to write an essay for the Betty Crocker Homemaker of Tomorrow Award. Without questioning the assignment, we did it. On scholarship awards day, I was horrified when my name was called as the award recipient. I wasn't even enrolled in home economics classes!"

As an adult, she continues to recognize behaviors that are viewed through a gendered lens. "We had a situation where a woman turned people off. It wasn't because of what she was saying or that it wasn't important. It was how she said it. I don't think that's a gender issue per se. It's human nature. But, when men can get away with the same behavior—that is a gender issue. People make allowances for men. They also provide more support for them when it comes to responsibilities like hosting social events [in an official capacity] and preparing food for them. I was expected to provide these services, my male counterparts weren't."

True to her upbeat nature, however, she suggests that this type of expectation is a door that swings both ways. "Women have an advantage that men don't have. It's just being a woman. There's nothing better. Whether we are nurturing or not, it's the perception that women care more. It makes them seem credible because perception's a reality for many people.

"As a leader you must be credible to survive. Throughout my career I have been viewed as a credible person. It goes to trust, which is hard to gain but easy to lose. I tried to keep things as transparent and open as possible. I say what I mean and mean what I say. And yet, I don't know that I had the complete trust of everyone.

"This job would be incredibly hard if you weren't competent and politically savvy because the positive things you do don't necessarily accumulate, but the negative things do. The expectation is that you will give pats on the back and thank yous. When I returned to Standing Rock for visits, people told me how proud they are of me and that I am a role model. How wonderful it is to hear that kind of affirmation. But around here I began asking myself, who does that for me? Who gives me the thank yous? You have to be self-assured or you could easily engage in a pity party—wow, nobody appreciates me. You must believe in yourself. But even though self-confidence can get you there, it's credibility that keeps you there.

"I think intuition had a lot to do with my decision to retire; I just knew it was the right time. I wanted to retire while I was still young enough to have a life that wasn't always under a microscope and on call 24/7. I enjoyed my seven and a half years as president, but I realized that I was getting older and with age comes a natural slowing-down process. When I was younger, I didn't think about emotional and physical stamina. As an older person I do. My energy level is not what it once was."

Karen has come full circle. She grew up at Standing Rock and was educated and worked there. She ended her career teaching at and leading the premiere BIA institution. And today she has returned to Standing Rock. "I was a public servant at the federal or state level most of my career. I think being a civil servant is compatible with tribal values in that I took pride in being a good servant of the people and a good steward of the people's money.

"I don't miss being president. I don't miss the politics. I do miss seeing students. I do miss my colleagues. I realize that my job did not define who I am and I can live without it. I will continue to serve on the Presidents Board of Advisors for Tribal Colleges and Universities and the Haskell Endowment Association Board of Trustees and advocate for tribal colleges, and Haskell in particular. I will pick and choose consultant jobs very carefully. I do not want to be tied down. I like reading, cooking, gardening, and using my computer when I want to and having the freedom to pick up and go somewhere at a moment's notice. I love the solitude of being in the country again and seeing my home place just three miles east of here. For now, I am very content."

BIBLIOGRAPHICAL NOTES

Karen Gayton Swisher's story is the result of careful readings of interview transcripts; vitae; Haskell Indian Nations University websites; the university's strategic plan and self-study; articles posted to *LJWorld.com* by Dave Ranney, George Diepenbrock, and Sophia Maines; David Melmer, "Haskell's First Female President to Retire," *Indian Country Today* (June 5, 2006); "Nations Within," an interview in *Teaching Tolerance* (Fall 1997, 11–15); and Caroline Sotello Viernes Turner, "On Pathways to the Presidency," *Show & Tell* (2006, 12–15).

ELEVEN

THE ROAD LESS TRAVELED

THE ROAD TO THE college presidency is well established and traveled quite frequently, albeit mostly by White men. It is not a superhighway. It has forks, crossroads, hills, and detours. For men the signage provided by mentors and sponsors is reasonably clear. Mentors warn about the upcoming twists and turns, when to yield, and which gear is needed to get to the top of the hill. Sponsors point out the most important cultural sights along the way. In addition, spouses enable men to bypass the detours of competing family priorities, such as having babies, raising children, and keeping a household together.

For women the way is less well marked. A fork can lead women off the road altogether and away from the academy; the crossroads are often unmarked; the detours appear more often and can be longer; and the hills are steeper. And as they crest the top, women often encounter slippery slopes caused by the inclement weather of gender bias and, for women of color, racial discrimination.

The fork in the road for women (and for men as well) occurs early in their careers and has to do with having options that our women at the top did not have. Most of the women in this book are products of an era when acceptable career options for educated women were few. Several of our leaders admit they never made a conscious decision to seek the presidency. Barbara Douglass started down her career path by way of an "escape" marriage. Carol Harter entered administration via the happenstance of budget cuts at her institution. In an age where career options for women are more plentiful, and with a generation that is perhaps more economically driven, will women choose the academy and, ultimately, the college presidency? Several of our women at the top asked this question. The level of public scrutiny that seems inherent in today's college presidencies makes the job overwhelming at times. Martha Nesbitt says point-blank that higher education is losing talent to industry because money matters. Will this new generation opt for more lucrative and possibly less intense leadership positions in other industry sectors?

If women stay within the academy, they travel as either faculty or administrators. Crossroads for women in faculty lines intersect the road to the presidency at two distinct points. The first crossroad for women faculty is whether to move into administration or remain in faculty. All of the women in this book decided to go into administration after working in the faculty ranks. Gretchen Bataille, Karen Swisher, and Pamela Shockley-Zalabak did so after many successful years as academics, teaching and writing books in their chosen disciplines. The second crossroad for women who begin as faculty, and the single crossroad for women who begin as administrators, is whether to remain in less-demanding, second- or third-level administrative positions or to push for the presidency. These nine women chose to turn toward the presidency.

With the large number of administrative vacancies expected as Baby Boomers retire, Shockley-Zalabak is disappointed in the small numbers of women she sees applying for higher education leadership positions. To encourage interest among younger women, Douglass entreats current leaders to speak out more about the pleasures of the presidency rather than the pains. Betty Siegel counsels women to make careful decisions about their careers and to listen for their true calling in life. For if one takes the crossroad that leads to the presidency, these leaders tell us that it is the passion for the job, not the perks, that makes that choice worthwhile. The question that looms large is: will the next generation of women decide to embrace the long hours, challenges, and stress associated with the college presidency?

Detours abound, but having a family is probably the most challenging, and tempting, detour on the road less traveled. All but one of the women featured in this book have been married; several have been divorced; two of them, Howard-Golladay and Harter, compromised with commuter marriages while in the presidency. A number of them have children, but they tackled childbirth and child rearing long before facing the demands of institutional leadership. As Harter notes, today women are delaying having children until their mid-thirties, which can also be mid-career for many academics, a crucial time for considering a move into administrative leadership and onto the road toward the presidency. Stopping out at this point can derail any attempt at the presidency. No clear path exists that women can take where this particular detour is concerned. We question how long women will have to make a choice between babies and boardrooms. And, we wonder, can women find a way to take this detour and still make it to the top?

As they head to the top of the hill, the signals are different for men and women as well. For men the signs say, "Maintain Top Safe Speed." For women they read, "Slow Down; Speed Bumps Ahead." Men who maintain top speed are seen as ambitious and assertive; women are not. As García, Harter, and Howard-Golladay will tell you, women who move up the hill at top speed are seen as too direct, overbearing, or bitchy. Shockley-Zalabak and others note that the professional and personal behavior of women leaders is closely and constantly watched. What they wear and with whom they are seen, especially if they are single, is monitored, commented on, and gossiped about. Although men are watched, too, even their extreme behaviors are not judged as harshly or deemed as measures of their ability to lead. What male president was ever called an ice king or frumpy in his official evaluation? García adds that women and people of color must exhibit superior performance because they are likely to get only one opportunity to make it to the top. It takes energy and speed to reach the summit. As our higher education system faces increasing challenges, how can we change these different perceptions and expectations so that in the future more women leaders can put on the gas and reach the presidency?

As our male colleagues have demonstrated, mentors and sponsors are key to successful navigation, avoiding or lessening the impact of obstacles, and finding your way. Most of the women leaders in this book have benefited from "roadside assistance" provided by mentors, often men who have traveled the road and know where the obstacles lie. Early in her nursing career, Howard-Golladay had the support of a White male hospital administrator who believed in her talents, but also helped her face the political realities that existed at that time in her rural Alabama community. Douglass knows that "you can't go it alone," and seeks advice and finds renewal by connecting with her network of friends and mentors. García has created a support system of other college presidents she has met through her active participation in the American Council on Education, in addition to advisors both within and outside of higher education. Feeling herself alone at the top of the hill, Karen Swisher sought out other tribal college presidents and her male predecessors at Haskell. On the path to her presidency, Nesbitt encountered multiple setbacks.

She was a finalist for three presidencies in three years. Frustrated, she pulled off the road and parked until several years later when she encountered a chancellor who inspired her to get moving again.

Several women we interviewed suggested that women in leadership should be doing a better job of mentoring other women. Douglass comments that we need to make clear what the job entails. García advocates the founding of a national mentoring program. If the presidency is as demanding for men as it is for women, why do more men find time to mentor those who want to follow in their footsteps? Are the detours taken and the obstacles faced too formidable, too exhausting, too time consuming to afford women the luxury of time to mentor others?

Finally, even successful women, like Mamie Howard-Golladay and Karen Swisher, who have figured out how to neutralize gender bias or racial discrimination and use it to their advantage, have encountered their effects. Many of the women in the study faced the winds of obvious prejudice. For instance, early in Millie García's journey, a high school guidance counselor tried to dampen her ambition by telling her to consider becoming a secretary instead of going to college. Sexist male colleagues created a chilly climate at DeKalb Community College for Martha Nesbitt. Betty Siegel, who proved to her male colleagues at the University of Florida that women can balance career and family, later interviewed for a job she found out she would surely have gotten had she not been a woman. In Iowa, Gretchen Bataille took what could have been a career-ending stand against paternalism in girls' basketball and for Title IX. Carol Harter weathered strong storms of politics and budget cuts in her first presidency at SUNY at Geneseo but was run off the road near the finish line by the powerful, antifeminist political sandstorms in Nevada. Gender bias and racial discrimination continue to influence the cultural mind-sets of many Americans—perhaps not as overtly as in the past, but they persist just the same. And they persist in higher education, an environment supposedly open and accepting of difference.

In the future the forks in the road might seem less prominent, the crossroads better lit, the detours shorter, the hills easier to climb, and, as Northwesterners put it, the weather might "fine up." But for the women featured in this book, this is the road they traveled and some still traverse. These women have graciously shared their journeys so that those who choose to follow them might see the guideposts along the way more clearly.

TWELVE

PROJECT METHODOLOGY

T HE STORIES PRESENTED in this volume are part of an ongo-
ing qualitative research project begun in 2002 by a team of
women academics from a variety of disciplines, including business, education, sports, public administration, and hospitality.
We recognized, as various sources have documented, that despite
the progress of women in the general workforce, women continue to be underrepresented in each of our fields of study. Much
of the literature about and research on leadership has been written by and about men, primarily White men. In addition, leadership traditionally has been examined using male behaviors and
characteristics as the norm against which women are assessed.
The leadership literature presents mixed messages about
whether women leaders function differently from men who hold
comparable leadership positions. We posit that the issue is really
effectiveness rather than gender, and that effective leaders, male
or female, subscribe to similar beliefs about leadership and act
more similarly than differently when they enact those roles.

Our extensive investigation of the leadership literature in our
fields found the body of knowledge on leadership to be dis-
jointed, with some researchers investigating a particular approach to leadership (e.g., transformational leadership) and
others examining a completely different but equally important

aspect crucial to effective leadership (e.g., cognitive framing). Based on our assumption that effective leadership is not gender-specific, we synthesized existing literature into a series of nine tenets of effective leadership (see table 12.1). This created a basic structure about what we believe contributes to effective leadership.

Participants were purposely selected for their ability to inform the study (Lincoln & Guba, 1985; Merriam, 1998; Yin, 2003). These women were viewed as effective leaders using two general estimates of effectiveness: reputation among peers and longevity of experience. In addition, we strove for ethnic, geographic, and institutional diversity within each field. The women chosen for the study also had control over organizational budgets and more than five employees who reported directly to them.

Table 12.1 Nine Tenets of Effective Leadership

1. **Effective leaders are passionate about their organizations.** They exhibit extraordinary commitment not only to the organization but to its people as well.
2. **Effective leaders are reflective.** They are self-aware, self-disciplined, self-confident, and self-assured.
3. **Effective leaders are competent.** They possess the intelligence and mental capacity to get the job done.
4. **Effective leaders are great communicators.** They have their fingers on the pulse of the organization.
5. **Effective leaders understand the role culture plays in shaping the way they lead.**
6. **Effective leaders possess the physical and emotional stamina, energy, and resilience needed to persevere over the long term.**
7. **Effective leaders are focused yet forward thinking.**
8. **Effective leaders respect and value individuality.**
9. **Effective leaders possess credibility.** The building blocks of credibility are trust, integrity, and power.

Because leadership is affected by context, it is difficult to study a leader independent of context. Therefore, qualitative case study was chosen as an appropriate methodology for the project (Yin, 2003). Case study design enabled the researchers to compare the leaders across organizational types, looking for common threads and patterns in their responses (Babbie, 2001; Miles & Huberman, 1994; Yin, 2003). A semistructured interview protocol was developed and piloted before participant interviews (Lincoln & Guba, 1985; Miles & Huberman, 1994; Yin, 2003). Most of the interviews were conducted face-to-face and took two to four hours to complete. All were tape recorded and transcribed. Data were categorized systematically by themes and patterns of responses delineated by multiple researchers to ensure consistency and validity. Additional information pertaining to the leader and her organization was also gathered for the case studies via college documents, newspaper articles, and the Internet. Once the cases were written, the research team reviewed them, and each case was shared with its respective participant for accuracy and trustworthiness.

Although other reports of this research focus on the leaders' experiences in relation to the tenets of effective leadership, the work presented in the *Pathways to Leadership* series presents their individual and unique voices as they discuss their values and the events that have shaped them as leaders in their respective fields.

REFERENCES

Babbie, E. (2001). *The practice of social research* (9th ed.). Belmont, CA: Wadsworth/Thomson.
Lincoln, Y. S., & Guba, E. G. (1985). *Naturalistic inquiry*. Newbury Park, CA: Sage.

Merriam, S. B. (1998). *Qualitative research and case study applications in education.* San Francisco: Jossey-Bass.

Miles, M. B., & Huberman, A. M. (1994). *Qualitative data analysis* (2nd ed.). Thousand Oaks, CA: Sage.

Yin, R. K. (2003). *Case study research: Design and methods.* Thousand Oaks, CA: Sage.

INDEX

Addy, Cathryn, 25
African American female leaders,
    71–85
ambition: Bataille on, 9; Douglass on,
    22; García on, 38, 41; Harter on,
    66–67; Howard-Golladay on,
    71–72; Shockley-Zalabak on, 110;
    women and, 145–146
Amin, Idi, 23–24
Arizona State University (ASU), 42,
    135
athletics, Harter on, 57, 62

Bataille, Gretchen M., 6*f*, 7–19
Bennis, Warren, 116
Bergen, Evelyn, 131
Berkeley College, 37–53
BIA. *See* Bureau of Indian Affairs
Black Mountain Institute (BMI),
    67–68
boundary monitors, Siegel on, 119
Boyer, Ernest, 43
Brown, Betsy, 13
Bureau of Indian Affairs (BIA), 131

California State University, Domin-
    guez Hills, 50–51

Capital Community College, 28, 34
care: Douglass on, 27; García on, 37;
    Swisher on, 140
change: Bataille on,12–13; Douglass
    on, 28–29; García on, 44; Siegel
    on, 114–115, 119
civil rights, Bataille on, 16
Coles, Robert, 122
collaboration: García on, 45–46; How-
    ard-Golladay on, 76–77; Nesbitt on,
    91–92; Siegel on, 118–119; Swisher
    on, 137; women and, 2–3
Combs, Arthur, 115–116
commitment: Bataille on, 15–16;
    Douglass on, 25–27; García on,
    38–39; Harter on, 61; Howard-Gol-
    laday on, 83; Shockley-Zalabak on,
    101–111; women and, 2
communication: Douglass on, 29–30;
    Howard-Golladay on, 77–79,
    82–83; and leadership, 150*t*; Nesbitt
    on, 93–94; Shockley-Zalabak on,
    101–111; Siegel on, 115–116
community: Douglass on, 27; García
    on, 37; Howard-Golladay on, 79
competence: Bataille on, 15–16;
    García on, 48–49; and leadership,

2, 150*t*; Nesbitt on, 92; Shockley-
Zalabak on, 102, 105; Swisher on,
140–141
confidence: Douglass on, 31; García
on, 47; Howard-Golladay on,
84–85; Nesbitt on, 95; Swisher on,
136
credibility: Douglass on, 29; García
on, 46; Howard-Golladay on, 81;
and leadership, 150*t*; Nesbitt on,
92–93; Swisher on, 140
crises, Bataille on, 15
culture: Bataille on, 11; Douglass on,
27; García on, 42–43; Harter on, 57,
59, 61; Howard-Golladay on, 73–74;
and leadership, 150*t*; Nesbitt on,
90; Shockley-Zalabak on, 105;
Siegel on, 122; Swisher on, 131–132,
134–135

death: Howard-Golladay on, 78; Swisher on, 135–136
decision making: Bataille on, 16; Nesbitt on, 91, 93–94; Siegel on, 119;
Swisher on, 137
DeKalb Community College, 88–89
discrimination: Howard-Golladay on,
72, 75; Nesbitt on, 89; Siegel on,
124–125; Swisher on, 139–140;
women and, 147–148
diversity: Bataille on, 8, 13–14; García
on, 47, 50–51; Harter on, 63–64;
Howard-Golladay on, 71–85; Siegel
on, 114; Swisher on, 130
Douglass, Barbara, 20*f*, 21–35

education: García on, 40; Harter on,
58; Howard-Golladay on, 71–72;
Siegel on, 123; Swisher on, 130

Emerald Eagle Scholars, 12
Emerson, Ralph Waldo, 126
Entebbe, Uganda, 23–24
ethical leadership, Siegel on, 117–118,
120
Extra Mile Award, 29

faculty: Bataille on, 14; Douglass on,
28–29; García on, 44; Harter on,
57, 62–63; Howard-Golladay on,
82–83; Nesbitt on, 90
family: García on, 41, 49; Harter on,
64–66; Howard-Golladay on, 71;
Nesbitt on, 96–98; Shockley-Zalabak on, 109–110; Siegel on, 122–
123; Swisher on, 130–131; women
and, 145
financial issues: Howard-Golladay on,
81–82; Swisher on, 133–134, 136,
138. *See also* fund-raising
Forum on Contemporary Cultures
(FCC), 68
fun, Douglass on, 34
fund-raising: Bataille on, 14; Douglass
on, 31; Howard-Golladay on, 80

Gainesville State College (GSC),
87–99
García, Mildred, 36*f*, 37–52
Gardner, Howard, 115
glass ceiling, Bataille on, 18
Godwin, Gail, 114
GSC. *See* Gainesville State College
G-Tech, 80–81

Happy Hill Farm, 12
Harter, Carol C., 54*f*, 55–68

.